With his usual knack for providing both commentary and sermon material beneficial for preachers, Danny Akin has once again not disappointed. Readers of this volume will find excellent material for preaching through 1 Peter. An exceptional resource for pastors and teachers alike!

David L. Allen, distinguished professor of practical theology, dean of the Adrian Rogers Center for Biblical Preaching, Mid-America Baptist Theological Seminary

Danny Akin combines the mind of a theologian, the heart of a pastor, and the zeal of an evangelist as he writes this newest addition to the Christ Centered Exposition series, his commentary on 1 Peter. I believe it will stand the test of time and still speak for many years to come to preachers preparing sermons as well as to Christians who yearn to go deeper into the words of the apostle Peter. Peter writes to all Christians as "exiles dispersed abroad" making a difficult pilgrimage through a hostile world. Danny Akin's insights help make Peter's counsel and commandments vividly real in our twenty-first-century context.

Andrew M. Davis, senior pastor of the First Baptist Church of Durham, North Carolina, and the founder of Two Journeys Ministry; visiting professor of church history at Southeastern Baptist Theological Seminary; council member of The Gospel Coalition; former trustee of the IMB

When my dear friend Danny Akin writes anything on the Scriptures, you can know that both in its exposition and its explanation, it will be a tremendous help for the teacher and preacher of God's word. This commentary on First Peter is no exception and reflects both faithful exegesis for the reader and firm encouragement for the church.

James Merritt, host of Touching Lives broadcast and former president of the Southern Baptist Convention

Of the many helpful volumes in the Christ-Centered Exposition series, this may be my favorite. First Peter is a theologically profound New Testament book that poses some difficult challenges to even the most skilled exegete. Danny Akin masterfully expounds the book's primary truths in a manner that shows he has distilled the message of 1 Peter over many years. Rarely is such faithful exposition so beautifully devotional, so filled with practical application, so saturated with references to the Christian heroes of ages past, and so rich with allusions to the great hymns of our faith.

Charles L. Quarles, research professor of New Testament and Biblical Theology and Charles Page Chair of Biblical Theology at Southeastern Baptist Theological Seminary.

This is the perfect commentary for preaching, teaching, or leading a small group on 1 Peter. Akin's writing is clear, accessible, and inviting. His exegesis and theology are faithful to the scriptural witness. The message of 1 Peter is also applied to the readers simply and powerfully. Buy it, read it, and be strengthened in your faith.

Thomas Schreiner, associate dean for the School of Theology and the James Buchanan Harrison Professor of New Testament Interpretation and Professor of Biblical Theology at the Southern Baptist Theological Seminary

Dr. Daniel L. Akin, a consistently thorough theologian, amplifies the ancient biblical text of First Peter in ways that speak to contemporary concerns without muting the voice of the biblical writer. He insightfully turns the gem of Scripture so the reader discovers splendid facets of the biblical text in new and applicable ways. Ultimately, *Exalting Jesus in 1 Peter* in the Christ-Centered Exposition Commentary series is a biblical telescope written not simply to be looked at but to be looked through in response to those thirstily crying out, "We would see Jesus!"

Dr. Robert Smith, Jr., Distinguished Professor of divinity at Beeson Divinity School, Samford University

CHRIST-CENTERED

Exposition

NT / COMMENTARY

AUTHOR Daniel L. Akin

SERIES EDITORS David Platt, Daniel L. Akin, and Tony Merida

CHRIST-CENTERED

Exposition

EXALTING JESUS IN

1 PETER

BRENTWOOD, TENNESSEE

Christ-Centered Exposition Commentary: Exalting Jesus in 1 Peter

B&H Publishing Group
Brentwood, Tennessee

ISBN: 978-0-8054-9700-7

Dewey Decimal Classification: 220.7
Subject Heading: BIBLE. N.T 1 PETER—
COMMENTARIES\JESUS CHRIST

Printed in the United States of America
1 2 3 4 5 6 7 8 9 10 • 30 29 28 27 26 25

SERIES DEDICATION

Dedicated to Adrian Rogers and John Piper. They have taught us to love the gospel of Jesus Christ, to preach the Bible as the inerrant Word of God, to pastor the church for which our Savior died, and to have a passion to see all nations gladly worship the Lamb.

—David Platt, Tony Merida, and Danny Akin
March 2013

AUTHOR'S DEDICATION

Dedicated to my four beautiful and godly daughters-in-law Ashley, Kari, Anna, and Kelsey. They are wonderful wives and mothers. They are true daughters of Sarah.

TABLE OF CONTENTS

1 Peter

ACKNOWLEDGMENTS

Words are not adequate to express my gratitude to Devin Moncada, Kimberly Rochelle, and Kim Humphrey for their invaluable assistance in my part of this commentary on First Peter. They are God's good gift to me.

SERIES INTRODUCTION

Augustine said, "Where Scripture speaks, God speaks." The editors of the Christ-Centered Exposition Commentary series believe that where God speaks, the pastor must speak. God speaks through His written Word. We must speak from that Word. We believe the Bible is God breathed, authoritative, inerrant, sufficient, understandable, necessary, and timeless. We also affirm that the Bible is a Christ-centered book; that is, it contains a unified story of redemptive history of which Jesus is the hero. Because of this Christ-centered trajectory that runs from Genesis 1 through Revelation 22, we believe the Bible has a corresponding global-missions thrust. From beginning to end, we see God's mission as one of making worshipers of Christ from every tribe and tongue worked out through this redemptive drama in Scripture. To that end we must preach the Word.

In addition to these distinct convictions, the Christ-Centered Exposition Commentary series has some distinguishing characteristics. First, this series seeks to display exegetical accuracy. What the Bible says is what we want to say. While not every volume in the series will be a verse-by-verse commentary, we nevertheless desire to handle the text carefully and explain it rightly. Those who teach and preach bear the heavy responsibility of saying what God has said in His Word and declaring what God has done in Christ. We desire to handle God's Word faithfully, knowing that we must give an account for how we have fulfilled this holy calling (Jas 3:1).

Second, the Christ-Centered Exposition Commentary series has pastors in view. While we hope others will read this series, such as parents, teachers, small-group leaders, and student ministers, we desire to provide a commentary busy pastors will use for weekly preparation of biblically faithful and gospel-saturated sermons. This series is not academic in nature. Our aim is to present a readable and pastoral style of commentaries. We believe this aim will serve the church of the Lord Jesus Christ.

Third, we want the Christ-Centered Exposition Commentary series to be known for the inclusion of helpful illustrations and theologically driven applications. Many commentaries offer no help in illustrations, and few offer any kind of help in application. Often those that do offer illustrative material and application unfortunately give little serious attention to the text. While giving ourselves primarily to explanation, we also hope to serve readers by providing inspiring and illuminating illustrations coupled with timely and timeless application.

Finally, as the name suggests, the editors seek to exalt Jesus from every book of the Bible. In saying this, we are not commending wild allegory or fanciful typology. We certainly believe we must be constrained to the meaning intended by the divine Author Himself, the Holy Spirit of God. However, we also believe the Bible has a messianic focus, and our hope is that the individual authors will exalt Christ from particular texts. Luke 24:25-27,44-47 and John 5:39,46 inform both our hermeneutics and our homiletics. Not every author will do this the same way or have the same degree of Christ-centered emphasis. That is fine with us. We believe faithful exposition that is Christ centered is not monolithic. We do believe, however, that we must read the whole Bible as Christian Scripture. Therefore, our aim is both to honor the historical particularity of each biblical passage and to highlight its intrinsic connection to the Redeemer.

The editors are indebted to the contributors of each volume. The reader will detect a unique style from each writer, and we celebrate these unique gifts and traits. While distinctive in their approaches, the authors share a common characteristic in that they are pastoral theologians. They love the church, and they regularly preach and teach God's Word to God's people. Further, many of these contributors are younger voices. We think these new, fresh voices can serve the church well, especially among a rising generation that has the task of proclaiming the Word of Christ and the Christ of the Word to the lost world.

We hope and pray this series will serve the body of Christ well in these ways until our Savior returns in glory. If it does, we will have succeeded in our assignment.

David Platt
Daniel L. Akin
Tony Merida
Series Editors
February 2013

1 Peter

What a Great Salvation Our God Has Given Us: Twelve Bedrock Truths of a Christian Salvation

1 PETER 1:1-12

Main Idea: God has orchestrated a hope that sustains suffering believers.

I. **God Saves Us through the Work of the Triune God (1:1-2).**
II. **God Saves Us through His Abundant Mercy (1:3).**
III. **God Saves Us for a Living Hope through the New Birth (1:3).**
IV. **God Saves Us through the Resurrection of Jesus Christ (1:3).**
V. **God Saves Us for an Incorruptible Inheritance in Heaven (1:4).**
VI. **God Saves Us and Keeps Us through Faith by His Power (1:5).**
VII. **God Saves Us for a Salvation Fully Realized at the End of Time (1:5).**
VIII. **God Saves Us to Rejoice Even When We Have Trials (1:6).**
IX. **God Saves Us and Sends Trials to Test the Genuineness of Our Faith (1:7).**
X. **God Saves Us So That We Can Love Jesus Unseen (1:8-9).**
XI. **God Saves Us through a Gospel Revealed to the Prophets (1:10-12).**
XII. **God Saves Us by a Gospel That Amazes the Angels (1:12).**

"Amazing Grace" is one of the most well-known Christian hymns in the world. Its lyrics uncover the heart and soul of the Christian faith:

> Amazing grace! How sweet the sound
> That saved a wretch like me!
> I once was lost but now am found,
> Was blind but now I see.
> (Newton, *Baptist Hymnal*, 104)

Salvation from sin through the blood atonement of Jesus Christ and his bodily resurrection is the core of Christianity. As Jesus claims about himself in Luke 19:10, "The Son of Man has come to seek and to save the lost." The Lord Jesus Christ, the eternal Son of God, came from heaven to earth on a rescue mission to save us.

Salvation, which Hebrews calls "such a great salvation" (Heb 2:3), is a theme that spans the entire New Testament. Passages addressing this "great salvation" specifically include John 3:1-18; 2 Corinthians 5:14-21; Romans 3:21-31; Galatians 4:1-7; Ephesians 2:1-10; and Titus 3:4-7. We find another in the opening words of 1 Peter. The book was written by the apostle Peter (1 Pet 1:1), a fisherman who lived along the Sea of Galilee. His father was named Jonah (Matt 16:17), and he had a brother named Andrew, who was also an apostle (Matt 10:1-4). Peter's name was originally Simon, until Jesus gave him the name Peter, meaning "rock" (Mark 3:16; also Matt 16:16-18). Peter was the leader of the twelve apostles, which is indicated by his name always appearing first in any list of the twelve disciples (Matt 10:2; Mark 3:16; Luke 6:14-16). Although he denied Jesus three times on the night of Jesus's betrayal (Mark 14:66-72), he was restored by our Lord (John 21:15-19), would preach the great Pentecost sermon (Acts 2), figures prominently in Acts 1–12, and would write two letters in our New Testament. Church tradition says Peter was crucified upside down in Rome in the latter days of the reign of the evil emperor Nero (AD 54–68).

Peter writes this letter from Rome as conditions are worsening for Christians across parts of the Roman Empire. "Babylon" in 1 Peter 5:13 is a symbolic reference to Rome. The time is around AD 62–63. The letter's recipients are believers, whom Peter calls "chosen . . . exiles" (1:1). They are scattered across five Roman provinces in what is now modern-day Turkey. The theme that rings out throughout the five chapters and 105 verses is hope in the midst of suffering (see 4:12-13). Rejoice when you suffer for Jesus because the glory of your salvation is on the way!

Now, what better way to prepare Christians for the "fiery ordeal[s]" (4:12) that are on the way than to remind them of the wonderful salvation they have in Jesus? This salvation gives a "living hope" (1:3) that will strengthen believers and sustain them no matter what trials and sufferings they may face.

In 1 Peter 1:1-12 we discover twelve bedrock truths of Christian salvation. I hope your breath will be taken away with what J. I. Packer called "the master theme of the Christian gospel . . . rescue from jeopardy and misery into a state of safety" (*Concise Theology*, 146).

God Saves Us through the Work of the Triune God

1 PETER 1:1-2

Peter is an "apostle," a sent one, of Jesus Christ, the promised Messiah of the Holy Scriptures. He has great concern for God's people wherever they live. In this instance, Peter directs his attention toward "those chosen, living as exiles dispersed abroad" in five Roman provinces (v. 1). The NASB says they are "strangers, scattered." In 1 Peter 2:11 Peter calls them "strangers and exiles," "sojourners and pilgrims" (NKJV). This world is not their home, and neither is it our home, for "our citizenship is in heaven" (Phil 3:20). Don't get tied down to this world! It is only temporary, and it pales in comparison to where we are going.

In verse 2 Peter highlights each member of the triune God and their work in our salvation. First, we are elect, chosen "according to the foreknowledge of God" (cf. Eph 1:3-6). Warren Wiersbe exegetes this verse clearly:

> This election was not based on anything we had done. . . . Nor was it based on anything God saw we would be or do. God's election was based wholly on His great grace and love. We cannot explain it (Rom 11:33-36), but we can rejoice in it. (*Be Hopeful*, 19–20)

God the Father's foreknowledge does not mean he only saw in advance that we would choose him. That would make salvation dependent on us. Foreknowledge is the wonderful truth that the omniscient God has always known us and set his grace and love on us for all eternity. It is a deeply intimate and personal knowing (Rom 8:28-29). In our experience of salvation, this foreknowing becomes a reality to us. Those God foreknows will believe, and those who believe are foreknown. The mysteries of divine sovereignty and human responsibility are beautifully wedded for our worshipful mediation and amazement.

Peter moves to the sanctifying work of the Holy Spirit. The word *sanctification* means to set apart. Sometimes in the New Testament, sanctification is our *position* in Christ that takes place at salvation. At other times, sanctification is our *progress* as we grow in Christlikeness (1 Thess 4:3) by the work of the Holy Spirit. Positional sanctification appears here in 1 Peter 1:2. We have been set apart to God at conversion, via regeneration, to "an inheritance that is imperishable, undefiled, and unfading, kept in heaven" (v. 4).

Peter says the effect of our election and sanctification is for us "to be obedient and to be sprinkled with the blood of Jesus Christ." Tom Schreiner connects this verse with the covenant in Exodus 24:3-8 as the background of Peter's idea:

> The blood of the covenant signifies the forgiveness and cleansing the people needed to stand in right relation with God. We see, then, that entrance into the covenant has two dimensions: the obedient response to the gospel and the sprinkling of blood. . . . Believers enter the covenant by obeying the gospel and through the sprinkled blood of Christ, that is, his cleansing sacrifice. (*1, 2 Peter*, 56)

Our salvation is gloriously Trinitarian. The Father elects, the Spirit sanctifies, and the Son cleanses. The Father initiates, the Spirit applies, and the Son accomplishes.

> Praise God from whom all blessings flow; . . .
> Praise Father, Son, and Holy Ghost.
> ("Doxology," *Baptist Hymnal*, 668)

In light of this amazing salvation, Peter interjects a quick prayer of encouragement: "May grace and peace be multiplied to you." Given that unmerited favor (grace) and true wholeness (peace) of life flow in our direction from such a great God, we can rest assured that they will come in overflowing abundance no matter what may lie ahead.

God Saves Us through His Abundant Mercy

1 PETER 1:3

Verses 3-12 are one, long, single sentence in the original Greek text. Peter has laid the foundation for our salvation in the triune God in the previous two verses. Now, he explores the marvels of this salvation like a jeweler inspecting the multiple facets of a magnificent diamond. Peter begins with a word of praise and worship.

"Blessed be the God and Father of our Lord Jesus Christ." Why is God to be "blessed" or praised (NIV)? Because of his mercy? Not quite! Because of his "*great* mercy" (emphasis added). Paul tells us in Ephesians 2:4 that God "is rich in mercy, because of his great love that he had for us." Grace is God giving us what we *do not* deserve. Mercy is God withholding from us what we *do* deserve. Lamentations 3:22-23 teaches us, "The steadfast love of the LORD never ceases; his mercies never come to an end; they are new every morning; great is your faithfulness" (ESV). God is kind and compassionate in the face of our sin. We deserve eternal punishment. He could choose to condemn us, and he would be just in doing so, but instead our great God chooses to forgive us in mercy.

God Saves Us for a Living Hope through the New Birth

1 PETER 1:3

God's great mercy produces something wonderful: the new birth. The electing, sanctifying, cleansing, and merciful God has created a new you and a new me by the new birth (see John 3:3,7). This act of "borning us again," or better, "borning us *anew*," is singularly his work. We did nothing to produce our physical birth, and we do nothing to produce our spiritual birth. As John 1:13 makes clear, those in Christ "were born [again], not of natural descent, or of the will of the flesh, or of the will of man, but of God."

The new birth also comes with a gift. Peter calls it a "living hope." The word "hope" appears here for the first of five times in Peter's letter (1:3,13,21; 3:5,15). It is a living hope, a "confident expectation, a joyful anticipation" (Lusko, *Through the Eyes of a Lion*, 97). Vaughan and Lea provide precious insight into the reality of this dynamic and active hope that we have. They write,

> We tend to take hope for granted, but it is well to remind ourselves that the pagan world of apostolic times (like the pagan world of our day) was a world without hope (Eph. 2:12). Unprecedented depression had settled over the masses. Life was care-ridden and full of worry. (*1, 2 Peter*, 19)

Christ, however, steps in and fills the believer's life with hope through the new birth.

God Saves Us through the Resurrection of Jesus Christ

1 PETER 1:3

The resurrection of Jesus Christ from the dead is the foundation of Christianity. No resurrection? No Christianity. It would be nothing more than a mirage, a myth, a fable. Peter and Paul are at one on this cardinal and nonnegotiable truth (1 Cor 15:3-6). The tomb is empty. Many witnesses saw him. Women witnessed him first. Neither the Romans nor the Jews could disprove the gospel proclamation that "he is risen." Because

Christ is resurrected and alive, we can be "born again." Because Christ is resurrected and alive, we have a "living hope."[1]

God Saves Us for an Incorruptible Inheritance in Heaven
1 PETER 1:4

The future for the Christian is bright. In this section, Peter draws his language from the books of Deuteronomy and Joshua. What we call the Old Testament would have been the only Bible Peter knew. What Israel received from God when they entered the promised land was only an inkling, a foretaste, of what we receive in Christ. Peter gets so excited that he piles up the descriptions of our future "inheritance." He lists four. Again, Vaughan and Lea serve us well as our teachers:

1. **It "can never perish."** The Greek word was occasionally used with a military connotation—of a land not ravaged by (or beyond the reach of) enemy armies. Sometimes it was used of a land unscathed by natural calamities. Likely the language here suggests perpetuity: the Christian's heritage is imperishable, not liable to corruption or decay. In short, death cannot reach and destroy it.
2. **It "can never . . . spoil."** The idea is that it is unpolluted, unstained by evil; it is beyond the reach of evil and cannot be contaminated by it. As the first term spoke of perpetuity, this speaks of purity and perfection. The inheritance lasts forever and forever retains its integrity.
3. **It "can never . . . fade."** That is to say, the Christian inheritance is not subject to the wasting effects of time. The root word was used of the withering of flowers, of the wasting of one's features by illness or age. The word used in the text suggests then a beauty that time does not impair or cause to wither away. It is unchanging.
4. **It is "kept in heaven."** This means that it is divinely preserved and therefore completely safe. The Greek word has the connotation

[1] For more on the resurrection of Jesus, see "The Resurrection of the Great King" in Daniel L. Akin, *Exalting Jesus in Mark*, Christ-Centered Exposition Commentary (Nashville, TN: Holman), 359–68.

> of being watched over or guarded, and then of being preserved (protected from loss or injury). The inheritance is not simply stored safely away (the idea of a similar word used in Col 1:5), but securely kept under God's careful watch. The readers may endure much hardship and suffering, but they can be sure that their eternal inheritance is secure, for it is in the custody of their God. His eye is ever upon it. (*1, 2 Peter*, 21)

No earthly inheritance matches our heavenly one. Nothing comes close.

God Saves Us and Keeps Us through Faith by His Power

1 PETER 1:5

Once more we observe the beautiful dance between God's sovereignty and man's responsibility. Salvation is secure, sure, and certain because God's power guards us. Jesus reaffirms this truth in John 10:27-30 when he says,

> *My sheep hear my voice, I know them, and they follow me. I give them eternal life, and they will never perish. No one will snatch them out of my hand. My Father, who has given them to me, is greater than all. No one is able to snatch them out of the Father's hand. I and the Father are one.*

Salvation is the work of God from beginning to end. He is the "author and finisher" (KJV), the "pioneer and perfecter of our faith" (Heb 12:2 CSB). However, we are not passive bystanders. We are not robots, "mere automations" (Schreiner, *1, 2 Peter*, 64). We persevere in faith, giving evidence of the genuineness of our faith. As the witty North Carolina evangelist Vance Havner quipped, "Faith that fizzles before the finish was faulty from the first." God's power protects us, and he uses persevering faith to do it. A saving faith gets us started, and a sustaining faith keeps us going. Both are God's gift and involve our participation.

God Saves Us for a Salvation Fully Realized at the End of Time

1 PETER 1:5

Christian salvation has three tenses: past, present, and future. God saved us from a deserved penalty and caused us to be born again. He currently sanctifies us and frees us from the power of sin. He will rescue us from sin forever and make us glorified like him.

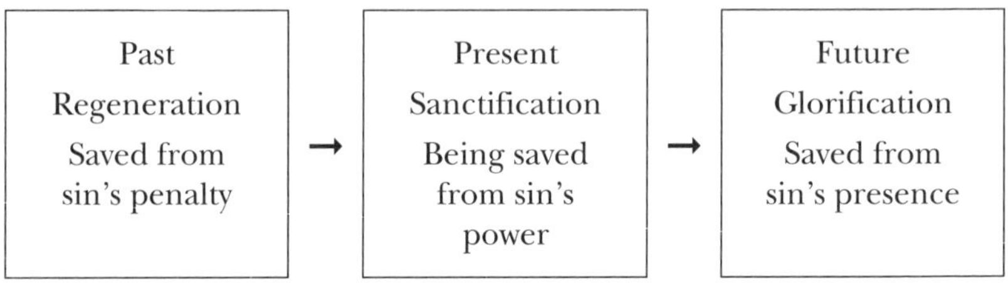

In verse 5, Peter writes about future salvation, a salvation that is ready to be revealed in the end times. A day is coming when our salvation will be full, complete, and publicly displayed for all to see. On that day we will see Jesus and be conformed to his perfect likeness (1 John 3:2). This salvation is imperishable, kept in heaven, and guarded by God. As E. E. Hewitt so wonderfully wrote,

> When we all get to heaven,
> What a day of rejoicing that will be!
> When we all see Jesus,
> We'll sing and shout the victory.
> ("When We All Get to Heaven," *Baptist Hymnal*, 603)

God Saves Us to Rejoice Even When We Have Trials

1 PETER 1:6

Salvation from sin, Satan, self, and all that's in the world is indeed cause for rejoicing. A future inheritance that is safe, secure, and on the way is more than we could hope or even imagine. Yet, following Jesus is not always easy or without difficulties. Our Lord himself told us that we must deny ourselves, take up our cross, and follow him (Mark 8:34).

Peter takes an honest and fair look at the Christian life in the here and now. "For a short time, if necessary," we may "suffer grief ["been grieved" ESV] in various trials." The NIV says, "all kinds of trials." Trials are an important part of our sanctification, our growing in likeness to Christ. As Paul writes, "We know that affliction produces endurance, endurance produces proven character, and proven character produces hope" (Rom 5:3-4). Trials are the rigorous exercises that strengthen our spiritual muscles. James provides similar counsel: "The testing of your faith produces endurance," which will enable us to "be mature and complete, lacking nothing" (Jas 1:3-4). We will suffer trials of various sorts. All are providentially and divinely allowed for our good (Rom 8:28). Simon Kistemaker says it well: "The trials which the believer experiences come from God's hand. These trials, in whatever form they appear, are ordained by God" (*Peter*, 46). Indeed, they come to us from the heart and hands of our loving, grace-filled, merciful heavenly Father. They are temporary, and they are for our good and his glory.

God Saves Us and Sends Trials to Test the Genuineness of Our Faith

1 Peter 1:7

Peter told us in verses 5-6 that we can expect trials in this life in anticipation of our salvation that we will experience "in the last time." Now he informs us of one of the reasons God sends trials and testing into our lives: they test the "proven character," the "genuineness" (ESV) of our faith. Peter compares our faith to gold and sufferings to fire. Real and authentic faith, he writes, is "more valuable than gold which, though perishable, is refined by fire." Is your faith real? Trials will prove it. Do you really trust Christ? The challenges, difficulties, and trials of this life will bring it to light for all to see. Faith purified in the fire of trials will shine bright today and forever (Dan 3). Further, this true and genuine faith will have eschatological consequences. It will "result in praise, glory, and honor at the revelation of Jesus Christ." This praise, glory, and honor are part of the believer's reward, but our faith ultimately contributes greatly to the worship of King Jesus (Schreiner, *1, 2 Peter*, 68). No wonder the apostles in Acts 5:41 could rejoice that "they were counted worthy to be treated shamefully on behalf of the Name." Ours is a little pain for a little while. His is great praise forever.

God Saves Us So We Can Love Jesus Unseen

1 PETER 1:8-9

In John 20 the Bible records three resurrection appearances of Jesus. The first is to Mary Magdalene (John 20:11-18). The second is to the disciples minus Thomas (John 20:19-23). The third is to all the disciples with Thomas present (John 20:24-29). Thomas had said, "If I don't see the mark of the nails in his hands, put my finger into the mark of the nails, and put my hand into his side, I will never believe" (John 20:25). When Jesus appears to Thomas, the disciple responds with one of the greatest Christological confessions in all of the Bible: "My Lord and my God!" (John 20:28). Interestingly and significantly, Jesus does not praise him. He mildly rebukes him: "Because you have seen me, you have believed. Blessed are those who have not seen and yet believe" (John 20:29). I believe this event is behind Peter's beautiful parallel affirmation in verse 8:

> *Though you have not seen him, you love him;*
> *though not seeing him now, you believe in him.*

As Paul writes in 2 Corinthians 5:7, "We walk by faith, not by sight." These dispersed believers had never seen the Savior, and neither have we. However, we have a sure and certain word in apostolic, eyewitness, gospel proclamation (2 Pet 1:19-21). Therefore, we love him, we believe in him, and we rejoice in him "with inexpressible and glorious joy." We cannot explain it all; we simply know that our faith is real and transcends far beyond what human words can describe. Seeing can wait; it is on the way (1 John 2:3). The hope of a future salvation of our entire selves (body and spirit) sustains our faith today.

Paul puts it exactly right in 2 Timothy 1:12: "I know whom I have believed, and am persuaded that he is able to keep that which I have committed unto him against that day" (KJV). Oh,

> Blessed assurance Jesus is mine!
> Oh, what a foretaste of glory divine.
> ("Blessed Assurance, Jesus Is Mine," *Baptist Hymnal*, 446)

God Saves Us through a Gospel Revealed to the Prophets

1 PETER 1:10-12

The coming of the Messiah did not spring out of nowhere. It had been promised and prophesied for centuries. A messianic thread is woven throughout the Old Testament, beginning just after Adam and Eve sinned in the garden of Eden:

Scripture		Messianic Promise
Genesis 3:15	→	Offspring of Woman
Genesis 12:1-3	→	Offspring of Abraham
Genesis 49:9-10	→	Tribe of Judah
Deuteronomy 18:15	→	Prophet Greater than Moses
2 Samuel 7:12-17	→	Greater Davidic King
Psalm 2	→	God's King
Psalm 16	→	Resurrection
Psalm 22	→	Crucifixion
Psalm 23	→	Good Shepherd
Psalm 110	→	King/Priest
Isaiah 7:14	→	Virgin Born
Isaiah 9:6-7	→	King with Four Names
Isaiah 52:13–53:12	→	Suffering Servant of the Lord
Daniel 7:13-14	→	Apocalyptic Son of Man
Micah 5:2	→	Birthplace Is Bethlehem
Zechariah 12:10	→	The Son of Israel Pierced

The promised One would be a Deliverer, a Savior, and the prophets could not take their eyes off of him. "Concerning this salvation," this "grace" that was to be theirs and ours, the prophets "searched and carefully investigated" ("searched intently and with the greatest care" NIV). Both *who* it was and *when* he would come occupied their hearts and minds. Further, "the Spirit of Christ," the Holy Spirit, predicted the *what*: "the sufferings of Christ and the glories that would follow." Peter H. Davids comments,

> The prophets could speak about this time which they did not understand because it was "the Spirit of Christ" who was in them giving testimony (or witnessing). . . .
>
> They did know however, that their prophecy would be fulfilled in a "distant age." (*First Epistle of Peter*, 62, 64)

Peter declared to the "chosen . . . exiles" that the promised day had come, and they were the recipients of it. Yes, "it was revealed to them" (v. 12), and in that act "they were serving not themselves but you." The prophets promised it, and the exiles are seeing the fulfillment of that promise. Peter effectively declared, "It's Now! Today! The promise of the Messiah is fulfilled and is now being announced through the preaching of the gospel." The idea that this was announced "to you by the Holy Spirit sent from heaven" almost certainly is a reference to Acts 2 and the day of Pentecost. The new has come. The old has been fulfilled. The gospel is now to be proclaimed to all without distinction.

God Saves Us by a Gospel That Amazes the Angels

1 PETER 1:12

Peter tells us that the things concerning the coming of the Messiah, his sufferings and glories, the preached gospel are "things into which angels long to look" (ESV). *The Message,* with a helpful paraphrase, says, "Do you realize how fortunate you are? Angels would have done anything to be in on this." The angels see all of redemptive history. However, they do not experience it the way we do. They are not the recipients of the grace of God and salvation the way we are. We were once lost; now we are found. We were blind; now we see. The angels have no such experiences. Nevertheless, they cannot take their eyes away from watching the drama of redemption unfold day after day, week after week, month after month, year after year, century after century. John Piper writes,

> If angels get excited about our salvation, how much more should we. If angels love to look at the work of God in saving sinners like us, how much more should we who are the very beneficiaries of that salvation (not just onlookers) love to look into it and be thankful for it and say with Peter, "Blessed be the God and Father of our Lord Jesus Christ." ("What the Prophets Sought and Angels Desired")

Conclusion

Christian salvation is a many-splendored glory. We will spend all of eternity reflecting on it and all it encompasses. Yet, there is a beautiful simplicity to its majesty. Martin Luther, the sixteenth-century Reformer, captures that simplicity in words that appropriately bring this chapter to a close:

> Learn Christ and him crucified. Learn to praise him and, despairing of yourself, say, "Lord Jesus, you are my righteousness, just as I am your sin. You have taken upon yourself what is mine and have given to me what is yours. You have taken upon yourself what you were not and have given to me what I was not. (*Letters I*, 12)

Hallelujah! What a Savior! Hallelujah! What a Salvation!

Reflect and Discuss

1. What does Peter mean by "chosen . . . exiles"? How does the label "chosen . . . exiles" shape how believers view themselves and one another? How would an exile identity change how you live?
2. How does remembering the gospel prepare Christians to suffer?
3. What does it mean to "get tied down to this world"? How do Christians live wisely without becoming tied to the world?
4. How does knowing that God saves you and sustains your faith cause you to depend on him?
5. Why do Christians forget how *great* God's mercy is? How can believers help one another to remember God's great mercy?
6. How is hope the center of the Christian life? How should hope change every part of the Christian life?
7. Describe something other than God that you hoped would fix issues in your life (e.g., person, job, location). How did these temporary hopes perish, spoil, or fade? How is the hope Jesus provides better?
8. Why must Christians remember all three "tenses" of salvation—past, present, and future? Which part of salvation do you emphasize? Which do you underemphasize?
9. How does suffering refine a believer's faith? Does suffering automatically refine faith?
10. Why should suffering Christians think about the resurrection of Jesus?

The Evidence of Authentic Christianity

1 PETER 1:13-21

Main Idea: Christians express their hope of salvation by imitating their Father's holiness.

I. You Must Be Hopeful (1:13-14).
  A. Prepare your mind (1:13).
  B. Move on from your former life (1:14).
II. You Must Be Holy (1:15-16).
  A. Holiness is the essence of God's character (1:15-16).
  B. Holiness is the expectation of God's children (1:15-16).
III. You Must Be Reverent (1:17-21).
  A. God is an impartial Father (1:17).
  B. Christ is an incorruptible Redeemer (1:18-21).

In 1981 Old Testament scholar Walter Kaiser published his superb work *Toward an Exegetical Theology*. Kaiser anticipated the idolatry of casual, comfortable, and convenient Christianity that looks nothing like the genuine and vibrant faith we find in the New Testament. Would the apostles recognize what parades about in our day as "the faith that was delivered to the saints once for all" (Jude 3)? Kaiser pinpoints the problem when he says,

> The church and the Scripture stand or fall together. Either the church will be nourished and strengthened by the bold proclamation of her Biblical texts or her health will be severely impaired. (*Exegetical Theology*, 6)

Kaiser then diagnoses the problem of the modern church in America and around the world. Kaiser wrote in 1981, and yet his words are still sobering. We desperately need ears to hear his verdict:

> It is no secret that Christ's Church is not at all in good health in many places of the world. She has been languishing because she has been fed, as the current line has it, "junk food"; all kinds of artificial preservatives and all sorts of unnatural substitutes have been served up to her. As a result, theological

> and Biblical malnutrition has afflicted the very generation that has taken such giant steps to make sure its physical health is not damaged by using foods or products that are carcinogenic or otherwise harmful to their bodies. Simultaneously a worldwide spiritual famine resulting from the absence of any genuine publications of the Word of God (Amos 8:11) continues to run wild and almost unabated in most quarters of the Church. (Kaiser, *Exegetical Theology*, 6)

"Christianity lite" is a sham, a false Christianity. It cannot endure "the fiery ordeal[s]" of opposition, persecution, and suffering (1 Pet 4:12-19). Without being grounded and rooted in the rock-solid foundation of biblical truth, we will be like the fool who built his house on the sand (Matt 7:24-27). Difficulties and hard times will expose and destroy a faulty and fruitless faith.

Peter knows our faith needs a solid foundation. He also knows there is no better place to lay that foundation than on the gospel of Jesus Christ. In verses 13-21 Peter peppers us with three imperatives: be hopeful, be holy, and be reverent. With these three commands he gives us three essential ingredients of a healthy spiritual diet that produces healthy Christians ready for the battles we will face (3:15). Each act proves that our faith is real and that our confession is authentic.

You Must Be Hopeful

1 PETER 1:13-14

The word "[t]herefore" begins verse 13. It looks back to verses 1-12, where Peter teaches that we have a sure and secure inheritance in Christ that is imperishable, undefiled, and reserved in heaven (v. 4). This salvation was made possible by the work of our triune God (v. 2). This salvation captivated the minds of the prophets (v. 10) and amazes the hearts of angels (v. 12). Because we have such an awesome salvation, we have a responsibility. Peter says to set our hope fully on God's coming grace by preparing our minds and being self-controlled, or sober minded.

Prepare Your Mind (1:13)

Peter tells us to prepare our minds and be sober minded. The phrase "with your minds ready for action" is literally "gird[ing] up the loins of your mind" (KJV). Peter imagines a man who tucks in his long flowing robe in order to run or do strenuous work. Schreiner believes there may be an allusion to the exodus when Israel was getting ready to leave Egypt (*1, 2 Peter,* 78). Today we may say, "Let's roll up our sleeves and get to work."

The New Testament writers regularly emphasize the mind in the Christian life. Paul writes in Romans 12:2, "Do not be conformed to this age, but be transformed by the renewing of your mind." In Philippians 2:5 he says, "Have this mind among yourselves, which is yours in Christ Jesus" (ESV). Peter calls us to engage our minds. C. E. B. Cranfield is right when he says,

> Strenuous thinking, a necessity at all times in Christian Church, can seldom have been more urgently needed than to-day. . . . It is a pathetic feature of contemporary church life that there are still plenty in the pews who clamor for shorter and lighter sermons and bright and easy services, and not a few in the pulpits prepared to pander to popular taste. . . . Peter's slogan is a call for us to break the vicious circle, a call for sermons which teach, not merely entertain, and for church members who will not shirk the discipline of intellectual effort, a call to the strenuous but exhilarating adventure of trying to understand ever more and more deeply the Gospel. (*First Epistle of Peter,* 32)

We have a great salvation. So let's tighten the shoelaces of our minds and run toward our hope in Jesus.

Peter adds to the call to prepare the mind that we must be "sober-minded." We must be self-controlled, balanced in our thinking. Calvin calls it

> spiritual sobriety, when all our thoughts and affections are so kept as not to be inebriated with the allurements of this world. . . . [W]hen one plunges himself into these, he must necessarily become sleepy and stupid, and he forgets God and the things of God. ("Commentaries," 44)

Genuine and authentic Christianity requires a prepared mind, a mind that is immersed in the Word of God and the things of God.

Move on from Your Former Life (1:14)

Verse 13 contains the first imperative in our passage and the main charge of verses 13-14: "Set your hope completely on the grace to be brought to you at the revelation of Jesus Christ." Peter already mentioned Jesus's coming revelation in 1 Peter 1:7. A prepared and controlled mind will focus on the future coming of Christ. It will be heavenly minded so that it may be of earthly good. Future grace and future hope flow from a transformed mind. Further, this hope in the second coming of Christ enables us "as obedient children" to "not be conformed to the desires of your former ignorance." In our "BC life," before Christ, we lived like an animal. Before Christ, we lived foolishly and in bondage to our passions and desires, captive to our fallen and sinful nature. As lost people, we lived like lost people. That was the old us. We are now a new people through the second birth (1:3). As 1 Peter 2:9 proclaims, we have been "called . . . out of darkness into his wonderful light" (NIV). So live up to who you are, not down to where you used to be. Keep your focus on the truth. Jesus is coming again! This hope will keep you away from the gutter of a life you have left behind.

You Must Be Holy

1 PETER 1:15-16

We are to be "obedient children" (v. 14). Such a challenge implies something about our Father. Children long to be like their fathers; it is in their nature. Our Father (v. 17) longs for us to be like him too. What is our Father like? Holy. He is holy. The pattern for our holiness is the holy God himself.

Holiness Is the Essence of God's Character (1:15-16)

The word "holy" dominates verses 15-16, appearing four times. We are commanded to be holy, the second imperative in our passage. We have been "called" to be holy because our God is holy. The word "holy" means to be separate or be set apart. David Peterson writes,

> Throughout Scripture, holiness is preeminently a characteristic of God himself. The terminology is used to signify that God is wholly other, distinct and separate from everything that he has made, and different from the gods of human imagination. As the Holy One, he acts in judgment

> against human sin and its consequences. Remarkably, however, he also chooses to dwell amongst those whom he has redeemed. They are "sanctified" or made holy by God's manifesting himself to them, drawing them into a special relationship with himself and making provision for their sinfulness. The holy people of God are then called to live in a way that demonstrates the reality of their relationship with God and with one another. A pattern of sanctification is established for Israel under the Mosaic covenant that foreshadows the definitive work of Jesus Christ and the operation of the Holy Spirit for believers under the new covenant. Indeed, the notion of a holy God among a holy people in a holy place is "the enduring eschatological hope of the Scriptures."
>
> God's holiness is associated with his majesty, sovereignty and awesome power (e.g., Ex. 15:11-12; 19:10-25; Is. 6:1-4; cf. Rev. 4:8-11). As the one who is supreme over all, he is transcendent, exalted and different from everything he has made. He cannot be compared with the gods of the nations or be judged by human standards. God alone is holy in himself. ("Holiness," 544–45).

God and God alone is unfathomably glorious, utterly pure, and radically set apart from his creation. He is holy. He is holy in his person. He is holy in his providence. He is holy in his purposes. He is holy in all his plans and actions. Psalm 29:2 instructs us as to our proper response to our Holy God: "Ascribe to the Lord the glory due his name; worship the Lord in the splendor of his holiness."

Holiness Is the Expectation of God's Children (1:15-16)

The essence of our heavenly Father is holiness. It is natural that his children, who have his nature through the new birth (v. 3), will grow to look like him. Peter calls us "to be holy in all [our] conduct" (v. 15). Holiness should characterize how we think, talk, and act. Peter grounds this command in Old Testament Scripture. "Be holy because I am holy" appears in Leviticus 11:44-45; 19:2; and 20:7,26. Paul also addresses the theme of our holiness in 1 Thessalonians 4:7: "For God has not called us to impurity but to live in holiness." Jesus would add in Matthew 5:48, "Be perfect, therefore, as your heavenly Father is perfect." So, what is the heart and soul of this divine call to holiness? J. I. Packer helps us at this point:

> Holiness is the healthy growth of morally misshapen humans toward the moral image of Jesus Christ, the perfect man. Their growth is supernatural. It takes the sanctifying work of the indwelling Holy Spirit to effect it. (*Rediscovering Holiness,* 106)

Our pattern is Christ.

The work of Christ provides an additional and powerful motivation to live a life of holiness for the glory of God.

You Must Be Reverent

1 PETER 1:17-21

The third imperative in our passage appears in verse 17: "[C]onduct yourselves in reverence." In other words, fear God. Two themes orbit about Peter's command: the impartial judgment of our heavenly Father (v. 17) and the atoning work of Jesus Christ (vv. 18-21). They serve as motivations for a holy life.

God Is an Impartial Father (1:17)

We call on God as Father because we are his children (v. 14) through the new birth (v. 3). Our Father is perfect in his holiness. Because he is holy, he is also a fair and impartial judge, judging each person "according to each one's work." Schreiner notes,

> The relationship we have with God is both tender and awesome. . . . God is an "impartial" judge who does not reward people as one who plays favorites (cf. Acts 10:34; Rom 2:11; Eph 6:9; Col 3:25). (*1, 2 Peter,* 83)

Such a reality should rightly strike fear in the heart of every person. It should inspire the children of God to live good, faithful, and impartial lives themselves. It should motivate us to be holy during our "time living as strangers" in this life on this earth. We do not fit well in this world with its behaviors, priorities, and values. We are strangers and should be recognized as such. This world is not our home. We are citizens of heaven (Phil 3:20), where our true Father and Savior await our arrival.

Christ Is an Incorruptible Redeemer (1:18-21)

Peter returns to the doctrine of salvation in verse 18, giving special attention to the atoning work of Jesus Christ. Peter contrasts who we were in our lostness with who we are now in salvation. He also teaches what God did not ransom us with and what he did ransom us with.

Why should we live in reverent fear before a holy God who is an impartial judge? The cost of your redemption! "You were redeemed from your empty way of life inherited from your ancestors, not with perishable things like silver or gold, but with the precious blood of Christ" (vv. 18-19). There is a long line of sinners trailing back to Adam and Eve in Genesis 3. Sin passes down from generation to generation. It is an "empty way of life" ("futile ways" ESV). We worshiped the wrong gods, lived for the wrong goals and priorities, and were controlled by the base desires and passions of the flesh. Simply put, we were a lost mess. But God! In great mercy! (v. 3). Intervened and redeemed ("ransomed" ESV) you! *Redemption* is one of the most important theological terms in the Bible. Schreiner is again our helper when he writes,

> The term "redeem" (*lutroō*) and the word group recalls Israel's liberation from Egypt (Deut 7:8; 9:26; 15:15; 24:18). The term is also applied to the liberation of individuals (Pss 25:22; 26:11; 31:5; 32:7), and in Isaiah the return from exile is portrayed as a second exodus (Isa 41:14; 43:1,14; 44:22-24; 51:11; 52:3; 62:12; 63:9). In the Greco-Roman world those captured in war could be redeemed and slaves were often manumitted, meaning that their freedom was purchased. . . . Peter derives his conception from the Old Testament. (*1, 2 Peter*, 84)

Our sin was immense, so the payment must be great. Our sin was immense, so the Savior must be great. Slaves were set free by perishable silver and gold. Sinners are set free by the perfect Son of God and the blood of the Lamb.

"Unblemished and spotless lamb" looks back to the sacrificial system of the Old Testament, perhaps to the Passover of Exodus 12 (1 Cor 5:7). The theme of God's lamb runs all the way from Genesis to Revelation. It is rich and reaches its climax in the shed blood and sacrifice of the Son of God.

Scripture	Theme	Type of Christ
Genesis 22	God provides the lamb.	Abraham and Isaac
Exodus 12	The sacrificial lamb must be without spot or blemish.	Passover
Isaiah 53	The lamb is to be slaughtered.	The Suffering Servant of the Lord
John 1:29	The Lamb will take away the sins of the world.	Jesus
Revelation 5	The warrior Lamb is on the throne in heaven.	The Exalted Lord

The Lamb is Jesus the Christ (v. 19). Peter expands on the perfect atoning work accomplished with the precious shedding of the blood of Christ and his death on the cross.

As verse 20 informs us, the cross was not a disappointing accident. It was a divine appointment even before God spoke creation into existence. In eternity past, before God made Adam and Eve, before they sinned, God had planned the redemption of sinners by the perfect sacrifice of his Son. It "was foreknown before the foundation of the world but was revealed in the last times for you" (v. 20)—for us.

It was planned in eternity but revealed in history. It occurred "in these last times," the time of the Messiah Jesus between his first and second comings. And it was for us. It is for us that he came and died a bloody death on a Roman cross.

Verse 21 addresses the conclusion of the matter. Through our faith and trust in the accomplished work of Christ, we are believers in God, the God "who raised [Jesus] from the dead and gave him glory." Resurrection and glorification once again are brought together (v. 11). Therefore, we rightly place our "faith and hope" in this God, the God who raised his Son from the dead and glorified him in the most exalted manner (Phil 2:9-11).

So live in reverent fear in light of the impartial Father we have and the precious atoning blood sacrifice of his Son. To fail to do so is dangerous. It should strike fear in your heart and soul. John Piper sums it up:

> Therefore, if in our conduct we are tempted to act as though the preciousness and the permanence of the blood of Jesus were impotent to hold us back from sin, then we should fear. Because if our lives bear constant witness to the powerlessness of the blood of Jesus, then Jesus is not really our hope and joy. And we do not belong to him. And that is a fearful prospect. The sum of the matter is this: hope in the grace of God! And fear not hoping in the grace of God! Fear the behavior that would show you don't trust in the all-satisfying preciousness of the love of Jesus. ("A Sojourn on Earth in Confident Fear")

Conclusion

Blaise Pascal reminds us, "Misery induces despair. Pride induces presumption. The Incarnation shows man the greatness of his misery by the greatness of the remedy which he required" (Pascal, *Pensées*, 143).

A hopeful life, a holy life, a reverent life—they all go together. A hopeful life, a holy life, a reverent life will avoid the vanity of a counterfeit Christianity. Such a life is the proper response, the only response, to the precious, spotless Son of God. He bought us out of the slave market of sin by his precious blood. So, we sing,

> What can wash away my sin?
> Nothing but the blood of Jesus,
> What can make me whole again?
> Nothing but the blood of Jesus.
> ("Nothing but the Blood," *Baptist Hymnal*, 223)

Meditate on this, and go and live a genuine and authentic Christian life.

Reflect and Discuss

1. In what way is hope a gift from God *and* an act to practice?
2. What does a hope not completely set on God's grace look like? What substitute hopes do you often cling to?
3. Why must believers equip their minds?
4. How does a transformed mind create future grace and future hope?
5. Why must the new birth happen before you attempt to become an obedient child? What happens if you reverse this process?
6. Why is it remarkable that believers are children of a holy God?

7. Why should hope for the future lead to holiness now?
8. What type of reverence does Peter describe in verse 17? Why should reverence motivate a holy life?
9. Are you ever uncomfortable when Christian hymns mention blood? Why? How do verses 18-19 clarify why it is important to teach and sing about Jesus's shed blood?
10. John Piper writes, "But if our lives bear constant witness to the powerlessness of the blood of Jesus, then Jesus is not really our hope and joy." Why is this true?

Marks of a Healthy Spiritual Family

1 PETER 1:22–2:3

Main Idea: The new birth creates love for the spiritual family and the Bible.

I. We Will Love One Another (1:22-25).
- A. We need a purified soul (1:22).
- B. We need a sincere heart (1:22).
- C. We need the new birth (1:23).
- D. We need the living Word of God (1:23-25).

II. We Will Long for the Word of God (2:1-3).
- A. The word helps us rid ourselves of evil works (2:1).
- B. The word helps us grow in our salvation (2:2).
- C. The word helps us see that the Lord is good (2:3).

On the night Jesus would be betrayed by his disciples and arrested by the leaders of Israel, he would perform the act of a slave and wash his disciples' feet (John 13:1-17). He would teach them about being a servant and deliver one of the most important statements in all of Scripture:

> *A new commandment I give to you, that you love one another: just as I have loved you, you are also to love one another. By this all people will know that you are my disciples, if you have love for one another.* (John 13:34-35 ESV)

The Bible talks a lot about love. I suspect it does so because we are often not good at doing it. If we were good at it, we would not need to be reminded about it so often. Jesus addresses the two great commandments of loving God and loving our neighbor in Matthew 22:34-40. Paul devotes an entire chapter to love in 1 Corinthians 13. John famously teaches us that "God is love" in 1 John 4:7-21. Peter addresses the importance of love as the final of four commands in chapter 1. He adds a fifth command in 1 Peter 2:2.

Set your hope completely (1:13).
Be holy (1:15).

Conduct yourselves in reverence (1:17).
Love one another (1:22).
Desire the pure milk of the word (2:2).

Love for one another is an essential and distinctive mark of a Christian and a healthy church family. Another mark is a longing and passion for the Word of God and the gospel of Jesus Christ. A love for one another and a love for the Bible go hand in hand. It is impossible to truly love God's Word but not his people, and vice versa.

One way to define love is *giving ourselves away for the good of another.* I once heard it called *passion in action.* J. I. Packer grounds his understanding of love in the cross and says,

> God's love is an exercise of his goodness toward individual sinners whereby, having identified himself with their welfare, he has given his Son to be their Savior, and now brings them to know and enjoy him in a covenant relation. (*Knowing God*, 123)

Giving at great cost for another's good, without regard to oneself, is at the heart of what it means to love. What, then, are two essential marks of a healthy church family?

We Will Love One Another

1 PETER 1:22-25

God gives us the supernatural ability to love people we do not like, or at least people we find difficult. Sometimes we are in the same spiritual family, the same local church. Peter is sensitive to this reality and provides four keys that will unlock our hearts and allow love to flow out in every direction.

We Need a Pure Soul (1:22)

Peter commands us to love one another "since you have purified yourselves by your obedience to the truth." The words "since you have purified" translate a single, perfect-tense participle in Greek, which looks at an event in the past with results that continue into the present. Peter's point is this: your soul began a transformation process the moment you were converted, the moment you were born again (1:3). That process continues in your sanctification and growth in Christlikeness. Your "obedience to the truth," your faith in the gospel (Rom 1:5), continues its work in your life and enables you to have a "sincere brotherly love" for others. Such love is authentic because it emanates from a soul that has been purified and continues to be purified. The new birth changes us on the inside and gives a supernatural ability to love others without distinction.

We Need a Sincere Heart (1:22)

The theme of purity continues in verse 22. We need a pure soul. We need to be pure in all that we are. We also need a pure and sincere heart. Peter attaches his command to this idea when he writes, "Since . . . you show sincere brotherly love for each other, from a pure heart love one another constantly." Our love for one another should be free from hypocrisy. It must be fervent and alive with heartfelt passion and zeal. Warren Wiersbe writes,

> Not only is this love a spiritual love, but it is also a *sincere* love ("unfeigned"). We love "with a pure heart." Our motive is not to get but to give. There is a kind of "success psychology" popular today that enables a person to subtly manipulate others in order to get what he wants. If our love is sincere and from a pure heart, we could never "use people" for our own advantage.
>
> This love is also a *fervent* love, and this is an athletic term that means "striving with all of one's energy." Love is something we have to work at, just as an Olympic contestant has to work at his particular skills. Christian love is not a feeling; it is a matter of the will. (*Be Hopeful*, 45; emphases original)

We Need the New Birth (1:23)

Peter alluded to the effects of the new birth in 1:22. Now he affirms that the new birth ("you have been born again") is essential if we want to love one another. The new birth changes our heart, transforms our soul, and makes us brand-new. One evidence, probably the most important evidence, is that we love one another. David Helm is right: "The mark of the Christian life is love" (*1–2 Peter*, 66). It is not our theology, though that is important. It is not our politics, though that is important.

It is not our education, wealth, religious activities, or standing in the community—all of which are important. The issue is this: Do we show that we are born again by the way we love others? Do people say of us, "Look how they love others"?

Perhaps a word from an ancient Christian teacher name Aristides (c. AD 133) would be helpful for our careful reflection. Writing to Emperor Hadrian (AD 117–138) he says,

> Now the Christians trace their origin from the Lord Jesus Christ. And He is acknowledged by the Holy Spirit to be the son of the most high God, who came down from heaven for the salvation of men. . . . They have the commands of the Lord Jesus Christ Himself graven upon their hearts; and they observe them, looking forward to the resurrection of the dead and life in the world to come. They do not commit adultery nor fornication, nor bear false witness, nor covet the things of others; they honour father and mother, and love their neighbours; they judge justly, and they never do to others what they would not wish to happen to themselves; they appeal to those who injure them, and try to win them as friends; they are eager to do good to their enemies; they are gentle and easy to be entreated; they abstain from all unlawful conversation and from all impurity; they despise not the widow, nor oppress the orphan; and he that has, gives ungrudgingly for the maintenance of him who has not.
>
> If they see a stranger, they take him under their roof, and rejoice over him as over a very brother; for they call themselves brethren not after the flesh but after the spirit.
>
> And they are ready to sacrifice their lives for the sake of Christ; for they observe His commands without swerving, and live holy and just lives, as the Lord God enjoined upon them. (Kay, "Apology of Aristides," 276–77)

These are the evidence of a born-again believer!

We Need the Living Word of God (1:23-25)

I love the way the Bible talks about itself. Here, in 1 Peter 1:23, Peter says the Word of God is "imperishable" and "living and enduring."

The writer of Hebrews adds that it is "effective and sharper than any double-edged sword, penetrating as far as the separation of soul and spirit, joints and marrow. It is able to judge the thoughts and intentions of the heart" (Heb 4:12). It is this imperishable, living, enduring, and effective word that planted in us the "seed" of the new birth. This new life that has burst forth from this seed is a life that will remain forever because the Word of God remains forever. Peter quotes the prophet Isaiah in verses 24-25: "All flesh is like grass, and all its glory like a flower of the grass. The grass withers, and the flower falls, but the word of the Lord endures forever" (see Isa 40:6-8). Peter declares, "This word is the gospel that was proclaimed to you" (v. 25). Grass and flowers have a temporal life, or "glory." In time they wither and die ("fall"). But the imperishable, living, enduring, and effective "word of the Lord endures forever." And it is "this word," the word of the gospel ("good news"), that was proclaimed. *The Message* renders it, "This is the Word that conceived the new life in you." Peter loves the Bible! God uses it to save us. Not surprisingly, he has more to say about it in 2:1-3.

We Will Long for the Word of God

1 PETER 2:1-3

Although there is a chapter division here, Peter continues the argument he began in 1:22. The theme of the "word of the Lord" (1:23-25) and "the pure spiritual milk" of the Word (2:2 ESV) concern the teachings of the Bible. Peter also gives further evidence of what genuine love looks like (2:1). The second mark we will always find in a healthy church is a longing for the Lord and his Word. This longing produces tangible results outside (actions) and inside (attitudes).

The Word Helps Us Rid Ourselves of Evil Works (2:1)

If we allow love to flow from our hearts and if we soak in the Word of God, we will be compelled to put away or "rid" ourselves of sin. The comprehensive nature of this command is made clear by the word "all," which is used three times in 1 Peter 2:1. Peter identifies five sins:

1. **Malice**: a general word for evil, "the opposite of that which is good in character and beneficial." It is "moral evil in all its forms."

2. **Deceit**: cunning or craftiness, "the attitude that desires to get the better of another by cunning and deception . . . [a] two-faced attitude that deceives and hurts for personal gain."
3. **Hypocrisy**: describes someone who plays the actor and conceals his real goals and motives; "a man who meets with a face [and words] which is very different from his heart."
4. **Envy**: "displeasure produced by witnessing or hearing of the advantage or prosperity of others . . . the running-mate of hyprocrisy." It covets the good fortune of others and wants it for oneself.
5. **Slander**: speech that "disparages another . . . that deliberately assaults the character of another and usually takes place behind the victims back" (taken from Hiebert, *First Peter*, 110–12).

Peter commands us to rip these vices from our life like we would discard a filthy garment. They are to have no place in our lives or our churches because they stand in moral and spiritual opposition to love and the living and abiding Word of God.

The Word Helps Us Grow in Our Salvation (2:2)

Peter returns to the Bible with a new and beautiful image. He commands us, "Like newborn infants, desire the pure milk of the word." Just as babies crave the nourishing milk of their mother, we must crave the nourishment that can only come from the Word of God. It will keep us away from the malnourishment of malice, deceit, hypocrisy, envy, and slander (2:1). And it will provide the healthy nutrients we need "so that you may grow up into your salvation" (2:2). Our sanctification is in view. Here Peter has progressive sanctification in mind. Our souls grow in spiritual vitality and Christlikeness by the nourishment we receive from a steady, daily diet of the Word of God. We cannot grow by any other way! Desiring the Word on a daily basis is also evidence that you are saved. Lost people loathe the Word of God. Saved people love the Word of God. Charles Spurgeon writes,

> O my brethren, what can be better for informing the understanding than the Word of God? Would you know God? Would you know yourself? Then search this Book. Would you know time, and how to spend it? Would you know eternity,

> and how to be prepared for it? Then, search ye this Book. Would you know the evil of sin, and how to be delivered from it? Would you know the plan of salvation, and how you can have a share in it? This is the Book which will instruct you in all these matters. There is nothing which a man needs to know for the affairs of his soul, between here and heaven, of which this book will not tell him. Blessed are they that read it both day and night; and especially blessed are they who read it with their eyes opened and illuminated by the Divine Spirit. If you want to be wise unto salvation, select the Word of God, and especially the Spirit of God, as your Teacher. There is nothing else that is equal to the Bible for inflaming, sanctifying, and turning in the right direction, all the passions of the soul. ("The Best Thing in the Best Place," 410)

The Word Helps Us See That the Lord Is Good (2:3)

"The pure milk of the word" helps us mature in our salvation, a salvation that climaxes in our future glorification. As we grow in our experience of salvation, something else wonderful happens. We will have "tasted that the Lord is good." Peter quotes from Psalm 34:8. Psalm 34 is a psalm of David when he was going through a time of trial and difficulty, likely when he was fleeing Saul (1 Sam 21:10-15), who was trying to murder him. When those times come, "bless the LORD at all times" (v. 1), "boast in the LORD" (v. 2), proclaim his greatness and exalt his name (v. 3), seek the Lord (v. 4), "look to him" (v. 5), cry out to him and trust he will save you from all your troubles (v. 6). "Taste and see that the LORD is good" (v. 8). There is a perfect connection here. If we desire the pure milk of the Word, then we will taste that the Lord is good. We experience the goodness and kindness of God through his Word. God's powerful Word has the spiritual protein of lean meat and the delightful taste of an ice cream sundae. It is good for us and satisfying. Feast on the Word and you will spit out malice, deceit, hypocrisy, envy, and slander; none of it will be appealing to you.

Conclusion

At conversion we get our first taste of the goodness of the Lord Jesus. As Hebrews 2:9 reminds us, he tasted death for everyone so that we can taste only that which is beautiful, healing, healthy, nourishing, and sweet. He drank and tasted the bitter cup of God's wrath so that we can taste the sweet nectar of him and his salvation. What are you hungry for? What excites your spiritual taste buds? Taste the Lord! He is good. He will satisfy. He is what we have all been looking for all our lives.

Reflect and Discuss

1. What are common ways people speak about love? (E.g., I've *fallen in* love; I *love* chocolate; I'm *crazy* about her; The *magic* is gone.) Do these ideas support the definition of love as "giving ourselves away for the good of another"? Explain.
2. Why can Peter *command* believers to love one another? What beliefs support his command to love?
3. Why should people who claim to be Christians but don't love God's people reexamine their new birth?
4. Why can you love other believers better when you remember that you are a family?
5. What harm occurs when believers love God's Word but not his people?
6. How do believers create sincere love for one another?
7. Why is the gospel displayed by believers loving one another?
8. Why does a lack of love produce malice, deceit, hypocrisy, envy, and slander?
9. How do malice, deceit, hypocrisy, envy, and slander malnourish the believer?
10. How does a desire for God's Word help you rid yourself of sin?

Who Are We in Christ?

1 PETER 2:4-10

Main Idea: God is creating a holy people through Jesus, the cornerstone.

I. We Are God's Spiritual House (2:4-8).
- A. We are living stones through Jesus (2:4-5).
- B. We are a holy priesthood through Jesus (2:5).
- C. We are an honored people through Jesus (2:6-8).
  1. Some are saved by Christ the living stone.
  2. Some will stumble over Christ the cornerstone.

II. We Are God's Spiritual People (2:9-10).
- A. We are a chosen race (2:9).
- B. We are a royal priesthood (2:9).
- C. We are a holy nation (2:9).
- D. We are God's people (2:9-10).
  1. We proclaim his praises (2:9).
  2. We receive his mercy (2:10).

"Who are we?" This is a fundamental question of our worldview. Unfortunately, many in the West (Europe and North America) are suffering an identity crisis when answering that question. Christians are not immune from this problem. With the advent of identity politics and intersectionality, perspectives that place our identity under the overarching categories of the oppressor and the oppressed, exactly who we are can become confusing, jaded, and false. In *Critical Dilemma,* Neil Shenvi and Pat Sawyer map out how the new religion of contemporary critical theory tells us how we should view the world.

Identity Marker	Type of Oppression	Oppressor Group	Oppressed Group
Race	Racism	Whites	People of color
Class	Classism	The rich	The poor
Biological sex	Sexism	Men	Women

Sexuality	Heterosexism	Heterosexuals	Homosexuals
Gender identity	Cisgenderism	Cisgender people	Transgender people
Physical/mental ability	Ableism	The able-bodied	People with disabilities
Age	Ageism/Adultism	Adults	The elderly/ children
Religion	Religious oppression	Christians	Non-Christians
Colonial status	Colonialism	Colonizers	Indigenous people
Skin color	Colorism	Light-skinned people	Dark-skinned people

Table 1. Oppressor/oppressed groups according to contemporary critical theory (*Critical Dilemma*, 96).

Shenvi and Sawyer then go on to reveal the stark contrasts that exist between a Christian worldview and a contemporary critical theory worldview.

Worldview Question	**Christianity**	**Contemporary Critical Theory**
Who am I?	A creature made in God's image	A member of various social groups locked in a struggle for dominance
What is the fundamental human problem?	Sin	Oppression
How can that problem be solved?	Redemption through Jesus	Activism and solidarity
What is my primary moral duty?	Glorifying God	Dismantling unjust systems and structures

How do I know the truth?	Revelation and reason	Lived experience
What is the end goal of history?	The new heaven and earth	Social justice

Table 2. Worldview questions answered by Christianity versus contemporary critical theory (*Critical Dilemma*, 282). Tables excerpted from: *Critical Dilemma*. Copyright © 2023 Neil Shenvi and Pat Sawyer. Published by Harvest House Publishers, Eugene, Oregon 97408. www.harvesthousepublishers.com

They make a simple, decisive observation that makes contemporary critical theory unsuitable for Christians. They write,

> For Christians, our primary identity is vertical. We first relate to God as his creatures and only secondarily to our fellow image bearers through family, friends, communities, and society at large. . . . According to contemporary critical theory, our primary identity is horizontal. We are part of various oppressed and oppressor groups locked in a struggle for dominance. (*Critical Dilemma*, 283)

The idea of oppressor-oppressed was well known to the first-century church. They lived with the boot of Rome on their neck. Slavery and sexism were the norms. Wealth and poverty were commonplace. There was no middle class. And the church struggled with Jew-Gentile relationships. That is why Paul would tell the Galatians, "There is no Jew or Greek, slave or free, male and female; since you are all one in Christ Jesus" (Gal 3:28). And that is why Peter points us to Christ for our identity. Horizontal relationships exist. But our ultimate identity is found in God. It is found in Christ. Jesus makes us one family. He makes us "a chosen race, a royal priesthood, a holy nation, a people for his possession" (1 Pet 2:9). Peter will pile up metaphors to describe the beauty of our identity in Christ. It is a glorious composite.

We Are God's Spiritual House

1 PETER 2:4-8

Peter writes to men and women, Jews and Gentiles, free and slave, poor and rich, young and old, citizens of Rome and noncitizens of Rome.

None of these labels sums up their true identity. No, they are those who "have tasted that the Lord is good" (2:3; Ps 34:8). They are those who have been "born again" (1 Pet 1:23)—the saved (2:2). However, there is much more to their identity in Christ. Peter unfolds this reality with rich imagery, repeatedly drawing from the Old Testament.

We Are Living Stones through Jesus (2:4-5)

In salvation, we come to Jesus by repentance and faith. Christ is described here as "a living stone" (v. 4). He is "living" because he is alive through his bodily resurrection (1:3,11,21). But God and lost humans have radically different opinions about this living stone. Peter alludes to Psalm 118:22, a prophetic psalm. Jesus is "rejected by people." The apostle John reminds us, "He came to his own, and his own people did not receive him" (John 1:11). Instead of embracing the Lord Jesus, they tossed him aside like broken pottery. In contrast, he is "chosen and honored by God" ("in the sight of God chosen and precious" ESV). God has given us his verdict about his Son, the Lord Jesus Christ, through his resurrection, ascension, and exaltation. The Father "highly exalted him and gave him the name that is above every name" (Phil 2:9). Martin Luther comments,

> [Peter] says in God's eyes the stone is elect, and an extremely precious stone; it is of great importance also that it takes away death, satisfies for sin, and rescues from hell, besides it freely gives us heaven. (*Commentary*, 87)

It is on the foundation of this "living stone," the one "chosen and honored" by God (v. 6), that we become "living stones" (v. 5). Schreiner writes, "Believers are 'living stones' because of their faith in the resurrected Christ. Jesus' resurrection life becomes theirs even while they live in the midst of a hostile world" (*1, 2 Peter*, 105). These "living stones," God's people, are not scattered about with no connection to one another. He fits them together so that they constitute a "spiritual house" (v. 5). Believers around the world make up the church, this spiritual house. It is spiritual because every stone and the whole house are indwelt by the Holy Spirit (1 Cor 3:16; 6:19-20). Paul makes a similar argument in Ephesians 2:18-22 when he explains that this house, the church, is a temple,

> *For through him we both [Jew and Gentile] have access in one Spirit to the Father. So, then, we are no longer foreigners and strangers, but fellow citizens with the saints, and members of God's household,*

> *built on the foundation of the apostles and prophets, with Christ Jesus himself as the cornerstone. In him the whole building, being put together, grows into a holy temple in the Lord. In him you are also being built together for God's dwelling in the Spirit.*

Every stone is unique. Every stone is valuable. Every stone has been chosen and placed in its location in Christ, the "chosen and honored cornerstone" of verses 6-7. We will see how great a builder God is once he finishes his work.

We Are a Holy Priesthood through Jesus (2:5)

God's spiritual house is still under construction. New stones are being added through missions and evangelism. Then those living stones are getting stronger by edification and discipleship. Peter intentionally mixes his metaphors to tell us why the spiritual house, the temple of the Holy Spirit, is "being built." The house is "to be a holy priesthood to offer spiritual sacrifices acceptable to God through Jesus Christ" (v. 5). We are both house (temple) and priests. All of us. Every single one. This verse is foundational to the doctrine of the priesthood of all believers. As believer-priests we all have direct access to God through our one mediator, the Lord Jesus Christ (1 Tim 2:5). Timothy George writes,

> The priesthood of all believers was a cardinal principle of the Reformation of the 16th century. It was used by the reformers to buttress an evangelical understanding of the church over against the clericalism and sacerdotalism [wherein priests have spiritual powers as mediators between God and man] of medieval Catholicism. . . . The reformers talked . . . of the "priesthood of all believers" (plural). For them it was never a question of a lonely, isolated seeker of truth, but rather of a band of faithful believers united in a common confession as a local, visible *congregatio sanctorum*. . . .
>
> The priesthood of believers is not a prerogative on which we can rest; it is a commission which sends us forth into the world to exercise a priestly ministry not for ourselves, but for others—"the outsiders," not instead of Christ, but for the sake of Christ and at His behest. . . .
>
> No one should deny the importance of the doctrine of the priesthood of all believers. It is a precious and irreducible part of our Reformation heritage and our Baptist legacy. But

> let no one trivialize its meaning by equating it with modern individualism or theological minimalism. It is a call to ministry and service; it is a barometer of the quality of our life together in the Body of Christ and of the coherence of our witness in the world for which Christ died. ("The Priesthood," 291–94)

Peter emphasizes ministry and service when he writes that as "a holy priesthood," we are "to offer spiritual sacrifices acceptable to God through Jesus Christ." This language echoes Romans 12:1-2 and Hebrews 13:15-16. It also connects with 1 Corinthians 10:31: "So, whether you eat or drink, or whatever you do, do everything for the glory of God." All that we do should be that which we can offer to God as spiritual sacrifices he will find acceptable. Warren Wiersbe provides helpful and practical counsel when he writes,

> In the Old Testament period, God's people *had* a priesthood, but today, God's people *are* a priesthood. . . .
>
> This means that our lives should be lived as though we were priests in a temple. It is indeed a privilege to serve as a priest. (*Be Hopeful*, 49; emphases original)

We Are an Honored People through Jesus (2:6-8)

Peter comes to his Old Testament scriptural basis for our status as living stones, a spiritual house, and a holy priesthood. He cites Isaiah 28:16; Psalm 118:22; and Isaiah 8:14. All three texts are prophetic of the coming Messiah. All three emphasize Christ as the stone.

Peter first references Isaiah 28:16 in verse 6: "For it stands in Scripture: See, I lay a stone in Zion, a chosen and honored cornerstone." Mount Zion is a synonym for Jerusalem, where our Lord was crucified and resurrected. He is the "cornerstone" (Eph 2:20). The cornerstone controls the lines of the building, ensuring that the walls are straight (Hiebert, *First Peter*, 126). "Christ is now seen as the key to all human destiny and the touchstone of all endeavor; faith in him leads to honour, unbelief to disaster" (Beare, *First Epistle of Peter*, 125).

Some are saved by Christ the living stone. Peter continues his quotation of Isaiah 28:16: "And the one who believes in him will never be put to shame." Believers will stand in Christ, accepted at the judgment. Peter reinforces this promise in verse 7 and says, "So honor will come to you who believe." Acceptance and honor before God are promises for all who trust in Christ and Christ alone. Calvin is right: "Christ is a precious stone in the sight of God; then he is such to the faithful. It is faith alone which reveals to us the value and excellency of Christ" ("Commentaries," 69–70).

Some will stumble over Christ the cornerstone. Peter quotes Psalm 118:22 in verse 7. Jesus applied the text to himself in Matthew 21:42. The stone was rejected by the Jewish leaders, Israel, and the Romans. The religious leaders thought they were building God's temple, his house, protecting the nation by their rejection of Jesus (John 11:50-51). But they rejected the cornerstone, the most important stone of all! In verse 8 Peter then quotes Isaiah 8:14. Not only is Jesus the cornerstone, he is "a stone to stumble over and a rock to trip over" for the unbelieving. By disbelieving and disobeying, they reject the stone (Christ), and God rejects them. Notice the human responsibility: "They stumble because they disobey the word." Notice God's divine sovereignty: "They were destined for this." God decrees the tragic end of unbelief just as he decrees the glorious end of faith. All is under his control.

We Are God's Spiritual People

1 PETER 2:9-10

Who are we in Christ? We are living stones, a spiritual house, and a holy priesthood. Peter will add to these, teaching that "as God's special people Christians are to minister as missionaries, proclaiming abroad the mighty acts of God" (Vaughan and Lea, *1, 2 Peter*, 48). Peter presents four images, which he draws from Exodus 19:5-6 and Isaiah 43:20-21.

We Are a Chosen Race (2:9)

We "are a chosen race." This phrase comes from Isaiah 43:20. The words would be striking to Jew and Gentile alike who once had such hostility, hatred, and animus toward one another. Christ tore down that wall and has made them one (Eph 2:11-22). John Piper is right: we are "chosen-from all the races" ("Christian Identity and Christian Destiny"). We are one unique spiritual race in King Jesus.

We Are a Royal Priesthood (2:9)

In verse 5 we are called "a holy priesthood." All believers are holy, set apart to God for priestly service to Christ and to one another. Now Peter adds that we are "a royal priesthood." Peter draws from Exodus 19:6, where the status was applied to Israel: "you will be my kingdom of priests." Now, God's royal priesthood is the church. As a royal priesthood believers belong uniquely to a king. That king is Christ. Kistemaker makes a connection to Zechariah 6:13 and the promise of Messiah as both a priest and king. He writes, "Zechariah prophetically portrays the Messiah as the royal priest; Peter reveals that believers are priests in a royal priesthood" (*Peter*, 92). Holy priests! Kingly priests! What a double honor we have.

We Are a Holy Nation (2:9)

Peter again looks to Exodus 19:6, calling the church "a holy nation." We are a special, specific, and united people set apart for service. Our service and loyalty do not belong to an earthly leader. We give total allegiance to a divine sovereign because we are bought by the precious blood of Christ (1 Pet 1:19). This allegiance to Christ put Christians in danger during the church's early days. Karen Jobes writes,

> Just as the understanding of Christians as forming a new people brought potential alienation from popular society, the potential conflict of loyalties brought charges of treason and poor citizenship upon Christians of the Roman Empire. Jesus' instruction to "give back to Caesar what is Caesar's and to God what is God's" (Mark 12:17) presents the issue of deciding which is which. First-century Christians were often persecuted and executed not because they worshiped Jesus—in a polytheistic society, what is one more god?—but because of the higher claim of the gospel that only in Christ is the one true God to be worshiped. Because the prosperity and welfare of the empire were believed to depend on religious forces, the Christian's exclusive allegiance to Jesus as God was naturally viewed as detrimental to the rest of society. From that perspective, Christians were bad citizens of the empire, and this made them subject to accusations of treason. The self-understanding of the early church as a holy nation is attested by the force brought against them by the Roman state. . . .
>
> Under the modern ideology that separates church and state, it is perhaps easier today to separate what belongs to Caesar from what belongs to God. But to the extent that government formulates policy directly bearing on moral and ethical issues (e.g., abortion, war, the place of religious faith

> in the public forum), Christians still have to face the problems raised by holding dual citizenship—in the country of their residence and in the holy nation of God. (*1 Peter*, 162)

To be a part of this "holy nation" is truly an honor and privilege. And it comes with inherent dangers and at potentially great cost.

We Are God's People (2:9-10)

The final descriptor is "a people for his possession." This phrase comes from Exodus 19:5 (see Deut 4:20; 7:6) and also Isaiah 43:20-21. In some ways this phrase brings together the various emphases of the previous three. The church is a different kind of people. All the earth and all peoples are God's. The church is his special people, "a people for God's own possession" (NASB) because of its blood-bought, born-again status. They are chosen, royal, holy, and God's unique possession. This amazing status comes with responsibilities and blessings.

We proclaim his praises (2:9). A holy, royal, and chosen people are called to be evangelists and missionaries. They are called to "proclaim the praises ["excellencies" ESV] of the one who called you out of darkness into his marvelous light" (see Col 1:13-14). God's special people are to declare to their neighbors and to the nations what their God has done for them through Christ. They are to proclaim the excellencies of the King who called them out of the darkness of sin and spiritual death into his marvelous light of forgiveness and the new birth. This light is wonderful because it is a light that gives life (John 1:4-5). The language echoes the creation account of Genesis 1:3-5. God effectually called us from darkness to light, from death to life, from Satan's kingdom to God's kingdom. This is a message we must herald to every tribe, tongue, people, and nation. This gospel is too good to keep to ourselves. Everyone is invited to become a part of this chosen race, royal priesthood, holy nation, and people of God. The missionary impulse is self-evident.

We receive his mercy (2:10). Peter closes this section drawing a contrast between our past and present status.

Once	Now
Not a people	God's people
Had not received mercy	Have received mercy

Our new status should cause us to praise the excellencies of our Savior and his salvation. Peter alludes to Hosea 2:23, showing this is a familiar pattern in how God relates to his people. Our status as God's people is not our doing. It is all of grace, all of mercy (1 Pet 1:3). And it is universal. Jew and Gentile alike are recipients of the marvelous mercy of God. "No people" are now "new people."

Conclusion

Jesus came to make us one. He came to make us a family. He came to make us one spiritual house, one chosen race, one holy nation. Carl Trueman is right: "Jesus did not need to be a woman to save women, or trans to save trans, or disabled to save the disabled. He simply needed to be human" ("When Identity Politics Consumes Theology"). We do not need to create a false Christ in our own image. We need the Christ who died and rose again to conform us to his image.

Reflect and Discuss

1. In what ways do people rely on themselves to define their identity? What are the problems with everyone defining their own identity?
2. If you define your own identity, what do you implicitly believe about authority, especially God's?
3. Compare the worldview questions in table 2. What different sources are used to answer these questions? How does the source for answers shape the outcome?
4. Why do Jesus and believers share an identity as "living stones"?
5. Being one stone of a spiritual house, why should you commit to a local church?
6. What relevance do external identity markers have for the church?
7. Why is the priesthood of believers a commission? What does a commission call us to do?
8. How is God's presence the goal and blessing of the believer's priesthood?
9. Read Romans 12:1-2 and Hebrews 13:15-16. What spiritual sacrifices can you offer to God? Why do these things please him?
10. What benefits come with each identity in verse 9 (a chosen race, a royal priesthood, a holy nation, and a people for his own possession)?

Who I Am Determines How I Live

1 PETER 2:11-12

Main Idea: Christian exiles avoid sin because it threatens their soul and because they want God to save others.

I. Know Who You Are (2:11).
   A. This world is not your home ("strangers").
   B. You are a visitor just passing through ("exiles").
II. Know How You Should Live (2:11-12).
   A. Abstain from sinful desires (2:11).
   B. Expect unfair criticism (2:12).
   C. Hope for evangelistic effectiveness (2:12).

The new birth (1 Pet 1:3), conversion, radically changes us. It gives us a new position *in* Christ, and it gives us new passions *for* Christ. Peter has beautifully painted a portrait of who we are and what we have in Christ in 1 Peter 1:1–2:10. Now he begins the second section of his letter (2:11–4:11), addressing how we live our new life every day. He will tell us how to respond to those in authority over us (2:13-25). He gives counsel on the husband-wife relationship (3:1-7). He will guide us on how to suffer well (3:8-22; 4:12-19). He will remind us about the second coming of Jesus, which should affect our lives now (4:1-11). What we have *in* Jesus (1:1–2:10) determines how we will live *for* Jesus (2:11–5:14). Verses 11-12 set the table for the specific instructions that will follow.

Know Who You Are

1 PETER 2:11

First Peter 2:11 begins with "Dear friends" or "Beloved" (ESV). The word may signal a new section (cf. 4:12). However, the word bears more weight than this. "Dear friends" is probably an inadequate translation. Peter's readers are loved. A deep affection exists with Peter and, more importantly, with God. Believers in the five provinces described in 1 Peter 1:1 are lavishly loved by God. How do we know? These believers are

chosen by God (v. 1);
blessed to have God as Father (vv. 3,14);
objects of his mercy (v. 3);
recipients of a living hope (v. 4);
graced with an incorruptible inheritance kept in heaven (v. 4);
protected by God's power (v. 5);
saved past, present, and future (vv. 3-5);
called by God (v. 15);
ransomed from sin by the blood of Christ (v. 18);
born again (vv. 3,23);
blessed with the living and abiding Word of God (v. 23); and
blessed with the good news of the gospel (vv. 12,25).

He loves you and me! Because we are grounded in this amazing divine love with blessings overflowing, Peter can make his appeal to those who follow Jesus.

This World Is Not Your Home ("Strangers")

Peter begins with a word of encouragement. He "urges" his readers. He does not get in their face or pull the "apostle card," taking advantage of his apostolic authority. He could do this, but he comes alongside them and gently puts his arms around them. He reminds them of who they are. They are "strangers" ("sojourners" ESV; "foreigners" NIV). Schreiner notes this word and the next ("exiles") "recall Abraham's status as a sojourner" in Genesis 23:4 (*1, 2 Peter*, 119). This world has nothing permanent for us. Our home is in heaven, not on earth. Our address is in heaven, not on earth (Phil 3:20). We live life, recognizing we "do not possess the same privileges and rights as the citizens" of this world (Kistemaker, *Peter*, 95). We are resident aliens whose citizenship is elsewhere. This world should feel strange to you. If it doesn't, you are making yourself at home in the wrong place.

You Are a Visitor Just Passing Through ("Exiles")

There is no significant difference between the words *strangers* and *exiles*. Most scholars see them as synonyms. Yet a shade of difference may be present. *Exile* has the emphasis of "a temporary visitor, one just passing through a foreign land with no intention of becoming either a citizen or a permanent resident" (Vaughan and Lea, *1, 2 Peter*, 54). Taken together, the rhetorical impact is powerful. We are strangers, exiled in a foreign land, with no place to call home. As Hebrews 13:14 reminds us, "We do not have an enduring city here; instead, we seek the one to come." Indeed, we long for the new Jerusalem of Revelation 21:2. John Calvin puts it perfectly: "The children of God, wherever they may be, are only guests in this world" ("Commentaries," 78). One of my favorite songs as a boy was "When We All Get to Heaven." The second stanza of that hymn captures the heart of Peter's words in verse 11.

> While we walk the pilgrim pathway
> Clouds will overspread the sky;
> But when traveling days are over,
> Not a shadow, not a sigh.
> When we all get to heaven,
> What a day of rejoicing that will be!
> When we all see Jesus,
> We'll sing and shout the victory.
> (*Baptist Hymnal*, 603)

Pilgrims, know who you are. Now, know how you should live.

Know How You Should Live

1 PETER 2:11-12

Peter has established who we are: "strangers and exiles." Now he can exhort us how to live as foreigners in a strange world that is not our home. He gives two appeals: "abstain" (v. 11) and "conduct yourselves" (v. 12). A third, however, is implied at the end of verse 12 (let evildoers "observe your good works"). These three appeals are given in the context of a war that is engaged in our soul with fury (v. 11). Warren Wiersbe reminds us that we are "soldiers involved in a spiritual battle" (*Be Hopeful*, 56). This battle rages within us and on foreign soil.

Abstain from Sinful Desires (2:11)

We have been born again and are purifying our souls by obedience to the truth (1:22). Growth in Christlikeness (progressive sanctification) means that we "abstain from sinful desires," desires that "wage war against the soul." Our greatest battles do not take place outside of ourselves in the world. Our greatest battles take place inside of us, in our soul (Rom 12:2). Good and God-given desires get twisted and disordered because of sin that dwells within us. These "sinful desires" carry an all-out assault against us, a spiritual military campaign, with the goal of taking us down and defeating us in battle. And it is a battle! Peter calls us to act and to fight. We cannot let down our guard. We must engage the battle and engage it continually. I love the way Luther puts it:

> But what does Peter mean in that he says, abstain from the lusts that war against the soul? This is what he would say: You are not to imagine that you can succeed by sports and sleep. Sin is indeed taken away by faith, but you have still the flesh which is impulsive and inconsiderate: therefore, take good care, that ye overcome it. By strong effort it must be done; you are to restrain and subdue lust, and the greater your faith is, the greater will the conflict be.
>
> Therefore, you should be prepared and armed, and should contend with it incessantly. For they will assault you in multitudes, and would take you captive. (*Commentary*, 109–10)

John Owen wisely said, "Be killing sin or it will be killing you" (*Works*, 9). This is a fight to the finish. Do not think that when you win a battle you have won the war. This is a war you will engage in until you are with Jesus.

Expect Unfair Criticism (2:12)

Because we are not at home in this world, how we think, talk, and act will often not be appreciated. It will certainly not be applauded. If we are criticized or opposed, however, it should be because of our stand for Christ, not because we are sinful or rude! We need to be slandered as evildoers because of our testimony to Christ and an honorable life. Peter admonishes us, "Conduct yourselves [continuously] honorably among the Gentiles." The marginal reading of the CSB is helpful here: "among the nations" or "among the pagans." Live a godly and holy life among those who are lost (1:15-16). Show them Jesus in talk and walk. Schreiner again is on target when he writes,

> Peter did not summon believers to a verbal campaign of self-defense or to the writing of tracts in which they defend their morality. He enjoins believers to pursue virtue and goodness,

> so that their goodness would be apparent to all society. (*1, 2 Peter*, 122)

Live a life of attractive and beautiful Christlikeness. Let your personal and social behavior among unbelievers radiate the glory and goodness of our King, whom we represent in a foreign land. Paul would tell you to be a good ambassador for Christ (2 Cor 5:20). Wiersbe says, "Back up our 'talk' with our 'walk' . . . our good works must back up our good words" (*Be Hopeful*, 56).

Hope for Evangelistic Effectiveness (2:12)

The final phrase of verse 12, "the day he visits" ("the day of visitation" ESV), is debated. "The day he visits" could refer to divine judgment at the end time. Or it could refer to the salvation of Gentiles (pagans), whom God visits with personal conversion in this life. Both views have good arguments to support them. I would argue Peter references the salvation of unbelievers. Jesus promised this in Matthew 5:16: "In the same way, let your light shine before others, so that they may see your good works and give glory to your Father in heaven." Schreiner points out that, in the New Testament, people glorify God by believing in him (*1, 2 Peter*, 122). Some unbelievers, seeing our good works and hearing the gospel, will repent and trust Christ and give glory and praise to Christ. Yet our witness is not easy. For a time they will slander us and speak evil against us. Don't get discouraged. Don't quit. Don't give in. Remember that the work and word of the gospel are the power of God unto salvation (Rom 1:16). Not all will be saved but some will. Maintain a faithful witness no matter what. You may be delightfully surprised by what God does.

Conclusion

Because sin wages war with us, we must "be killing sin" as Owen famously said (see Rom 8:13). How do we "kill" sin? Grant Gaines has expanded on Owen's thoughts with nine instructions for killing sin. His words provide great wisdom as we bring this chapter to a close.

1. **Diagnose sin's severity.**
   When a person has struggled with a sin for a long time, it'll be more difficult to kill. This is especially the case if there have been long seasons when that person has indulged the sin rather than actively trying to kill it.

2. **Grasp sin's serious consequences.**
Even for the Christian, who has been declared righteous positionally, sin remains dangerous. . . . A Christian's sin grieves the Holy Spirit (Eph. 4:25-30), wounds the Lord Jesus (Heb. 6:6), and can cause a Christian to lose his or her usefulness for ministry.

3. **Be convinced of your guilt.**
Ask yourself, "Why have I gone on sinning when I've been shown such grace and mercy?"

4. **Earnestly desire deliverance.**
According to Owen, "Unless thou longest for deliverance thou shalt not have it."

5. **Consider the relationship between your sins and your natural temperament.**
Each person has a unique temperament and nature that make certain sins harder to kill. Owen reminds us, "A proneness to some sins may doubtless lie in the natural temper and disposition of men."

6. **Avoid occasions that incite sin.**
Consider the circumstances that attend your falling into sin, and guard yourself from them. . . . If we want to stop sinning, we must avoid the slippery places that occasion our falls.

7. **Address sin's first signs.**
We'll be most effective in putting sin to death when we "rise mightily against the first actings" of our sinful desires. . . . [I]t's hard to stop if we allow our desire for it to grow.

8. **Meditate on God's glory.**
We must not let [sin] gain ground. Instead, we must turn from our sin to "the excellency of the majesty of God." When we see God's glory, we'll see our sin's ugliness in contrast.

9. **Don't rush to comfort yourself.**
Though we may experience guilt and conviction over sin, we shouldn't assume the sin is defeated. Sin is deceitful, and it can trick us into thinking we've dealt with it decisively when we have not. ("John Owen's 9 Instructions")

Pastor Gaines then closes his article with an excellent summation:

> Sin is like an aggressive snake. If we don't proactively attack sin, it will prove deadly. Thankfully, we aren't alone in the fight. The power to kill sin comes from Christ through the Holy Spirit. As we focus on snuffing out sin, we must also draw near to the throne of grace. It's there we'll find grace to help in our time of need (Heb. 4:16). Effort is necessary, but as Owen says, "Mortification [the subjection and denial of sinful passions] of any sin must be by a supply of grace. Of ourselves we cannot do it." ("John Owen's 9 Instructions")

God has already rescued us from this world. Aim to live like an exile awaiting your future home.

Reflect and Discuss

1. Review the above twelve blessings of a believer. Why should who you are in Christ lead to a holy life?
2. Peter refers to exiles, plural. What will happen if a Christian attempts to live outside a community of believers?
3. Why must Christians urge one another to avoid sin? How can you do this?
4. What should Christians expect, since they "do not possess the same privileges and rights as the citizens of this world"?
5. Where else in the Bible do war metaphors refer to the Christian life? How can the war metaphor shape how you respond to sin?
6. How do Christians fight against sinful desires? Why do Christians have power to kill sin?
7. Will an end to difficult circumstances guarantee you have killed sin?
8. What may non-Christians find honorable about the Christian life? How can you excel in these areas so that others may glorify God?
9. What is the difference between a holy life and a superficially religious life?
10. Review the nine instructions for killing sin. What sin can you practice these on? Write down your thoughts and work through them with someone in your community.

God, Government, and the Christian

1 PETER 2:13-17

Main Idea: A God-focused obedience of authority is good and necessary.

I. **Submit to Divinely Ordained Authorities (2:13-16).**
   A. It is the will of God (2:13-15).
   B. It will provide a good witness (2:15).
   C. It reveals we are free in Christ and slaves to God (2:16).

II. **Respect and Honor Everyone (2:17).**
   A. Honor everyone.
   B. Love your Christian family.
   C. Fear God.
   D. Honor the earthly leader.

Civil disobedience—the refusal by people in a country to obey commands or laws of a government without resorting to violence—has a long and interesting history for the people of God. Being civil, it is nonviolent. And warrant for civil disobedience is easily located in the Bible. David Helm notes,

> All the preacher would need to do is turn up some of the great biblical passages that deal with this theme. He could tell of the Egyptian midwives who rightly disobeyed Pharaoh out of the fear of God; the gallant Shadrach, Meshach, and Abednego who doggedly refused to worship Nebuchadnezzar's statue out of reverence for Yahweh; Daniel, who faithfully refused to follow legislation that prohibited prayer to the Most High; finally, the preacher could wax eloquently on Peter and John, who stood defiant in the face of authorities when ordered to stop preaching in Jesus' name. (*1–2 Peter*, 89–90)

The Bible teaches there are situations when the people of God must say no to the government in order to say yes to God. As Peter and the apostles said in Acts 5:29 when they stood before the Sanhedrin, the

Jewish Supreme Court, "We must obey God rather than people." Yet, the general teaching of the Bible points us in a different direction.

The Bible's basic orientation is toward civil *obedience*, even when the governing authorities are ungodly and unjust. Nero (AD 54–68) was the emperor when Paul wrote Romans 13:1-7 and Titus 3:1-2 as well as when Peter penned 1 Peter 2:13-17. Peter will teach us that God's rationale for such a command is theological and apologetic. It honors the sovereign providence of God, and it helps our witness to the lost.

A biblical framework for government and Christians should provide our backdrop for reading 1 Peter. Daniel Heimbach argues the book of Daniel "provides more on God relating to sinners governing sinners than any other book in the Bible and does so in universal terms not affected by shifting politics" (*Fundamental Christian Ethics*, 412). He provides twenty-three biblical truths regarding Christians and the government.

1. God does not expect compliance with policies interfering with godliness (Dan. 1:8).
2. Godly people should respect those governing while avoiding compromise (Dan. 1:8; 6:21).
3. God controls all wisdom and power affecting government (Dan. 2.20).
4. God controls the rise and fall of political history (Dan 2:21).
5. God controls wisdom and knowledge needed by political advisors (Dan. 2:21).
6. God gives wisdom and power to political advisors who seek it from him (Dan. 2:23).
7. God knows what will happen and has a plan for political history (Dan. 2:28).
8. God controls whatever sovereignty, power, strength, and glory rulers have (Dan. 2:37).
9. God controls what rulers are able to rule (Dan. 2:38).
10. When pushed, godly people obey God rather than human rulers (Dan. 3:18,28; 6:10).
11. The sovereignty of God over human governing is everlasting (Dan. 4:3,35; 6:26).
12. The sovereignty of God over human governing is universal (Dan. 4:25,32; 5:21).

13. The sovereignty of God over human governing cannot be destroyed (Dan. 6:26).
14. God bestows ruling power on anyone he wants (Dan. 4:25,32; 5:21).
15. God wants rulers to accept being accountable to him for how they rule (Dan. 4:26).
16. No human governing limits God's supremacy over it (Dan. 4:35).
17. The sovereignty of God over human governing is eternally true and just (Dan. 4:37).
18. God never loses control and can always humble rulers who resist him (Dan. 4:37).
19. God sets himself against rulers who set themselves against God (Dan. 5:23).
20. The life breath of every human ruler depends on God (Dan. 5:23).
21. God controls the course in life taken by every human ruler (Dan. 5:23).
22. All should fear "the living God," including all human rulers and governments (Dan. 6:26).
23. God is able to rescue anyone out of the hands of wicked rulers (Dan. 5:27). (Heimbach, *Fundamental Christian Ethics*, 412–13)

This framework will help us as we consider Peter's counsel on this issue.

Submit to Divinely Ordained Authorities

1 PETER 2:13-16

The God of the Bible is the divine Sovereign of the universe. He has absolute authority over all things. In his providence he has established three institutions on earth: family, government, and church. He also has provided instruction for all three institutions. Government receives significant attention in Daniel; Romans 13:1-7; 1 Timothy 2:1-4; Titus 3:1-2; and 1 Peter 2:13-17. Jesus provides the foundation for how we interact with government in Matthew 22:21 when he says, "Give, then, to Caesar the things that are Caesar's, and to God the things that are God's." God has placed humanly ordained authorities under his kingship. And what is our responsibility to the divinely ordained authority of government? In a word: "submit."

Our world and even many Christians balk at the idea of submission. *Submission* is not a bad word; it is a biblical word. A quick survey of the Bible drives home this point.

- Jesus was submissive (and children are to be submissive) to his parents (Luke 2:52; Eph 6:1-3; Col 3:20).
- We are to be submissive to one another (Eph 5:21).
- Wives are to be submissive to their husbands (Eph 5:21-24; Col 3:18; 1 Pet 3:1-7).
- Christians are to be submissive to their church leaders (1 Cor 16:16; Heb 13:17).
- Slaves are to be submissive to their masters (Eph 6:5-8; Col 3:22-25; 1 Pet 2:18-20).
- Christians are to be submissive to God (Jas 4:7).
- The church is to be submissive to Christ (Eph 5:24).
- The Son in his incarnate state was submissive to the Father (John 5:19,30,36; 14:28).

Yet, many reject the idea of biblical submission for three main reasons. First, we live in a radically self-centered, self-autonomous age when the self is at the center of a person's life. Second, we do not have a biblical understanding of submission. Many assume submission implies inferiority. The Bible never teaches this. Third, some people abuse their authority, which drives others away from the biblical beauty of the idea.

What, then, is biblical submission? Nathan Foster, in his book *The Making of an Ordinary Saint*, writes,

> Submission is the spiritual discipline that frees us from the everlasting burden of always needing to get our own way. In submission we are learning to hold things lightly. We are also learning to diligently watch over the spirit in which we hold others—honoring them, preferring them, loving them. Submission is not age or gender specific. We are all—men and women, girls and boys—learning to follow the wise counsel of the apostle Paul to "be subject to one another out of reverence for Christ" (Eph. 5:21). We—each and every one of us regardless of our position or station in life—are to engage in mutual subordination out of reverence for Christ.
> The touchstone for the Christian understanding of submission is Jesus's astonishing statement, "If any want to become my

followers, let them deny themselves and take up their cross and follow me" (Mark 8:34). This call of Jesus to "self-denial" is simply a way of coming to understand that we do not have to have our own way. It has nothing to do with self-contempt or self-hatred. It does not mean the loss of our identity or our individuality. It means quite simply the freedom to give way to others. It means to hold the interests of others above our own. It means freedom from self-pity and self-absorption.

Indeed, self-denial is the only true path to self-fulfillment. To save our life is to lose it; to lose our life for Christ's sake is to save it (see Mark 8:35). This strange paradox of discovering fulfillment through self-denial is wonderfully expressed in the poetic words of George Matheson:

> Make me a captive, Lord,
>   And then I shall be free;
> Force me to render up my sword,
>   And I shall conqueror be.
> I sink in life's alarms
>   When by myself I stand;
> Imprison me within Thine arms,
>   And strong shall be my hand.

The foremost symbol of submission is the cross. "And being found in human form, [Jesus] humbled himself and became obedient to the point of death—even death on a cross" (Phil. 2:7-8). Now, it is not just a "cross death" that Jesus experienced but a daily "cross life" of submission and service. And we are called to this constant, everyday "cross life" of submission and service.

All the spiritual disciplines have the potential to become destructive if misused, but submission is especially susceptible to this problem. As a result, we need to be clear regarding its limits. The limits of the discipline of submission are at the points at which it becomes destructive. It then becomes a denial of the law of love as taught by Jesus and is an affront to genuine Christian submission. These limits are not always easy to define. Often, we are forced to deal with complicated issues simply because human relationships are complicated. But deal with them we must. And we have the assurance that the Holy

> Spirit will be with us to guide us through the discernment process. (*The Making of an Ordinary Saint*, 21–22. Excerpt from *The Making of an Ordinary Saint* by Nathan Foster, copyright © 2014. Used by permission of Baker Books, a division of Baker Publishing Group.)

God calls us to joyfully and willingly yield in our will to his divinely ordained authority. In the context of 1 Peter, it is the government. Being human, government clearly is not perfect. As John Calvin wisely put it, "Some kind of government, however deformed and corrupt it may be, is still better and more beneficial than anarchy" ("Commentaries," 83). God is ultimately sovereign over all government. Peter provides three reasons for us to submit to the government.

It Is the Will of God (2:13-15)

Peter admonishes us in 2:12 to live honorably among the nations so that we bear a good gospel witness. He will now begin to apply that teaching to various relationships in life. His directive about the government is straightforward: "Submit to every human authority." Why? "Because of the Lord." (v. 13). In this way we honor Jesus and his lordship over us. As I submit to governing authorities, I submit to the lordship of King Jesus. Peter then specifies in verses 13-14 the governing authorities with selective examples. We submit "whether to the emperor [or king] as the supreme [earthly] authority or to governors as those sent out by him." Keep in mind, there was no concept of modern democracy in the ancient world.

The governing authorities of the world have a clear assignment: they are "sent out by [the emperor] to punish those who do what is evil and to praise ["commend" NIV] those who do what is good" (v. 14). Schreiner writes, "Rulers help maintain order in society by commending good citizens" (*1, 2 Peter*, 130). Alan Stibbs says, "Such rulers have a divinely appointed responsibility to preserve law and order, to prevent anarchy and moral corruption, and to promote and encourage good conduct" (*First Epistle General*, 108).

We honor Christ by submitting to and honoring God-ordained authority in accord with "God's will" (v. 15). The only exception is if we are called to disobey and dishonor our God. Then and only then may we civilly disobey.

It Will Provide a Good Witness (2:15)

We submit to the government and its servants because it honors Christ and is the will of God. We also do it because we will "silence the ignorance of foolish people by doing good" (v. 15). We have one King: Christ! When we honor and obey him, we become better citizens, not worse. Wiersbe says it well: "God has willed that we silence the critics by doing good, not by opposing the authority" (*Be Hopeful*, 60). We muzzle our critics and silence the ignorant and foolish by "doing good," which includes obeying the law and our governing officials. Because of our radical allegiance to Christ as the true King, Christians potentially open themselves to the charge of sedition. Peter says to put such foolish talk to silence by good public conduct and by obeying the government. Further, be a blessing to the place where you live. Be known for your acts of charity and kindness. Don't separate from the people around you and live like a monk! Live a positive Christian witness among the lost. Care for orphans and widows (Jas 1:26-27). Help the poor (Prov 19:17). Rescue the weak, the needy, and the oppressed (Ps 82:3-4). Be known more for what you do and what you love and less for what you don't do and what you hate. Follow the example of Jesus and put the gospel on beautiful display for all to see!

It Reveals We Are Free in Christ and Slaves to God (2:16)

"Submit" is better than "live" in verse 16 in my judgment. The verb must be supplied because there is not one in the original Greek text. The CSB rightly picks up the main verb from verse 13. We "submit as free people" because we are free in Christ. Sin is no longer our master. Christ is. We are now "free to choose to live in a way that honors the God whom [we] serve before the eyes of a pagan society" (Jobes, *1 Peter*, 177). Calvin says, "It is a free servitude, and a serving freedom" ("Commentaries," 84). We have been set free from slavery to sin, Satan, and this world so that we can be slaves of our God. Freedom in Christ will not lead us to use our "freedom as a cover-up for evil." Freedom in Christ does not lead to indulging in sin but to glorifying God by doing good. Praise God that we now have the supernatural ability to do what we ought to do. Amazingly, what I ought to do now lines up with what I want to do! I want to serve my King Jesus with a life that puts on marvelous display his redeeming love and amazing grace. Pastor John Piper says it perfectly:

> What this verse teaches is that we belong to God and not the American government. We are slaves of God and not man (1 Corinthians 7:22-23). We do not submit to human institutions as slaves to those institutions but as God's free people. We submit in freedom for his sake. Not in bondage for the king's sake.
>
> God has transferred us in one profound sense from this age to the kingdom of his Son. We have passed from death to life. But then for a season he sends us back into this age, as it were, not as we were once—as slaves to sin and guilt and the whims of this age and its institutions—but as free people, as aliens who live by other values and other standards and goals and priorities. We do submit. But we submit freely, not cowering before human authorities, but gladly obeying our one true King—God.
>
> Our whole disposition of freedom and joy and fearlessness and radical otherness from this world is rooted in our belonging to God—which in one sense is slavery (because his authority over us is absolute) but in another sense is glorious freedom (because he changes our hearts so that we love doing what he gives us to do).
>
> As Martin Luther said in his wonderful little treatise called "The Freedom of a Christian": A Christian is a perfectly free lord of all, subject to none. A Christian is a perfectly dutiful servant of all, subject to all.
>
> The key to that paradox is God. Freed by God from slavery to all human institutions; and sent by God freely and submissively into those institutions—for his sake! ("Slaves of God")

Respect and Honor Everyone

1 PETER 2:17

Verse 17 is composed of four concise imperatives and serves as an appropriate conclusion. Schreiner notes, "Two of the commands remind us of Proverbs 24:21, 'Fear the Lord and the king,' though Peter reserves fear for God alone" (*1, 2 Peter*, 132). We will briefly examine the four statements. Vaughan and Lea note we may have two couplets: "Honor all men; love the brotherhood. Fear God; honor the king" (*1, 2 Peter*, 61).

Honor Everyone

We are commanded to honor everyone without exception. Honor begins and ends the verse. To honor is to show someone respect. We value them as image bearers of God and people for whom Christ died. They have worth, regardless of external considerations. Piper says, "The way you respect a scoundrel like Judas and the way you respect a saint like John will be different. But there is a way" ("Slaves of God").

Love Your Christian Family

Second, Peter says, "Love the brothers and sisters" ("brotherhood" ESV). We are called by God to love all people, including our enemies (Matt 5:44). But there is a unique and special love we are to have for the family of God. It is often said that blood is thicker than water, but Spirit is thicker than blood. We respect and honor all people, but there is a tender bond and familial love among Christians. Surprisingly Peter commands us to love. Perhaps there is a gentle reminder that some may not be lovable. We still strive to love them. They are family.

Fear God

This command recalls 1 Peter 1:17. Schreiner says, "Peter may have been taking a swipe at the emperor cult here" (*1, 2 Peter*, 133). If so, Peter reminds us to "fear" with reverent awe no one other than our Sovereign Lord and King. Adulations given to some politicians in our day are improper for believers. God belongs in a category of respect, awe, fear, and worship that rightly belongs only to him. He will accept no competition.

Honor the Earthly Leader

We have come full circle. We submit to the emperor, king, or president (v. 13). We honor the emperor, king, or president. We are commanded to pray for them in 1 Timothy 2:1-2. These commands are not only for the ones we like or agree with. It is for all of them. It may not be easy, but it is right. We may express disappointment and disagreement in countries where we have that right without fear of consequences. We must do it respectfully. We must avoid hatred, slander, misrepresentation, unkindness, and harshness. We represent King Jesus. His rule over your life should temper your tongue and hold back your fingers from the keyboard.

Conclusion

God ordains and establishes all governments. So we honor, respect, and obey them. But we give our allegiance to God, to the Savior who is our King. While we live as "strangers and exiles" in this world, there are some basic principles for how we think and act. Sam Storms has written "10 Things You Should Know about the Christian's Responsibility to Human Government."[2] His insights are worth quoting at length.

1. **All governmental authority comes from God (Romans 13:1,4,6).** Those in authority are therefore rightly called God's "ministers" (Rom. 13:4) and "servants" (Rom. 13:6). This is not referring to their spiritual condition. This is their function under God's sovereignty. They "serve" God and his purposes, even if they are oblivious to his influence over their lives.

2. **Because all governmental authority comes from God, all Christians are to live in subjection to it (Romans 13:1,5; 1 Peter 2:13-17).** That does not mean we must obey everything that our government commands or requires. There are certain exceptions.

3. **Because all governmental authority comes from God, to resist "it" is to resist God (Romans 13:2).** Simply put, a crime against the state is a sin against God. Our obedience to the law of the land is based first and foremost on principle: obedience to God, and only secondarily because of the consequences it may bring.

4. **The purpose of government (the state) is two-fold; first, to promote and praise good, and second, to punish and prohibit evil (Romans 13:3-4; 1 Peter 2:14).** It is not the purpose of the state to promote or preach the gospel, and we should oppose any law that seeks to utilize the state for that purpose. It is the responsibility of the Church to preach the gospel.

5. **Paul was not oblivious to the fact that sometimes governments do the very opposite: they promote and praise evil and punish and prohibit good.** The Apostle Peter knew what it was like

---

[2] I have made only slight adaptations to this excellent article.

to live under tyranny and barbarism. He lived and ministered during the reigns of the Emperor Augustus, Herod the Great (who ordered the slaughter of the male infants in and around Bethlehem in an attempt to kill the new-born Jesus), Herod Antipas (who executed John the Baptist and not only presided over the mock trial of Jesus but joined with the soldiers under his authority to torment and ridicule our Lord), Pontius Pilate, Herod Agrippa (who executed James, the brother of John, and arrested Peter with the intent of doing the same to him), and Nero.

6. **It is the right of government to levy taxes and the obligation of its citizen to pay them (Romans 13:6-7).** But also note that simply paying our taxes isn't enough; we must also show the respect and honor due unto the agencies and agents of the state for fulfilling their God-ordained responsibilities.

7. **Neither Paul nor any other biblical author ever endorses a particular form of government.** We must remember that the Roman state was pagan and dictatorial; yet Christians functioned and even flourished under it. Neither Paul nor any other biblical author knew anything of democracy. [As an aside, I do think democracy, though not perfect, is the best form of government in a fallen world.]

8. **Are Christians ever free to publicly criticize their government and its officials? Yes!** The church is the conscience of the state and therefore must call it to account when it fails to fulfill its role as God's minister for good. [This is the danger of the church aligning itself too closely with any government or political party. It loses its prophetic voice.]

9. **So, are Christians ever free to engage in civil disobedience? Yes.** Neither the authority given to the state nor the obligation of the Christian to obey it is absolute. The best example of this is in Acts 5:27-29. [We obey God over any human authority.]

10. **Under what circumstances or on what grounds may a Christian engage in civil disobedience? Answer: When the state prohibits us from doing what the Bible commands, or commands us to do**

> **what the Bible prohibits (again see Acts 5:27-29).** John Jefferson Davis provides us with some guidelines to determine when certain laws of the land demand that we disobey:
>
> First, "the law being resisted must be unjust and immoral, clearly contrary to the will of God," and not just inconvenient or burdensome.
>
> Second, "the legal means of changing the unjust situation should have been exhausted. Civil disobedience should be seen as a method not of first resort, but rather of last resort, when legal channels have already been pursued."
>
> Third, "the act of disobedience must be public rather than clandestine."
>
> Fourth, "there should be some likelihood of success, particularly when the intent is to produce changes in laws and institutions."
>
> Finally, "those who consider civil disobedience should be willing to accept the penalty for breaking the law." ("10 Things")

One day we will no longer worry about kings, governments, and presidents. There will be no need for them just as there will be no need for the sun (Rev 21:23). God will rule in his bright and glorious splendor as our amazing, saving, and righteous King. Until then, we honor God by honorably submitting to earthly rulers.

Reflect and Discuss

1. Pick one of the twenty-three biblical truths about Christians and government. What happens if a Christian removes this truth? What happens if a Christian believes this truth but excludes any of the others?
2. If the Bible's "basic orientation is toward civil obedience," then how should you think differently about your earthly authorities?
3. Describe the authorities you have. Do you avoid submitting to any? Do you dishonor any with your words?
4. Why is having earthly authorities good?
5. Describe the last time you talked or wrote about any authority. Did your words honor them? Could people glorify God because of your words?

6. Should Christians participate in politics? How can Christians be the "conscience of the state" without creating a Christian government?
7. How do you honor the Lord by submitting to divinely ordained authorities?
8. How does Jesus's death and resurrection prove that God controls evil authorities? What does God promise to Christians who suffer?
9. Does unrestricted freedom for people exist? Is unrestricted freedom good? How can restrictions be a blessing?
10. What motives push Christians to dishonor others? What can you change so that you honor others more?

I Have Decided to Follow Jesus

1 PETER 2:18-25

Main Idea: Suffering Christians imitate Jesus by enduring injustice without responding in an evil manner.

I. Submit to Those in Authority Even When You Suffer Unjustly (2:18-20).

A. Do good to those who treat you well (2:18).

B. Do good to those who treat you unjustly (2:18-20).

II. Follow the Example of Jesus When You Suffer Unjustly (2:21-25).

A. Christ suffered for us (2:21-23).

B. Christ was a substitute for us (2:24).

C. Christ is a Shepherd to us (2:25).

For most of my life I have been a member of churches that give a public invitation after the preaching of the Word of God. People are invited to publicly confess Jesus as Lord and Savior, present themselves for baptism or church membership, rededicate their lives to Christ, or simply to come and pray. The "walk the aisle invitation" can be abused or misunderstood when given poorly. But countless lives have changed through a public invitation when it is extended with care and sensitivity. A popular invitation hymn is "I Have Decided to Follow Jesus." The four stanzas are simple, clear, and convicting.

> I have decided to follow Jesus;
> I have decided to follow Jesus;
> I have decided to follow Jesus;
> No turning back, no turning back.
> Though none go with me, I still will follow;
> Though none go with me, I still will follow;
> Though none go with me, I still will follow;
> No turning back, no turning back.
> My cross I'll carry, till I see Jesus;
> My cross I'll carry, till I see Jesus;
> My cross I'll carry, till I see Jesus;
> No turning back, No turning back.

> The world behind me, the cross before me;
> The world behind me, the cross before me;
> The world behind me, the cross before me;
> No turning back, no turning back.
> (*Baptist Hymnal*, 434)

The theme of following Jesus, especially in his suffering, is an important one in 1 Peter 2:18-25. It is the essence of discipleship (Mark 8:34-38). His "example" (1 Pet 2:21) is an aspect of his atoning work, but his example is not the heart of the atonement. The heart of the atoning work of Christ is penal substitution. Jesus, by his death on the cross, paid the penalty of our sins and died in our place. As verse 24 so beautifully says, "He himself bore our sins in his body on the tree." J. I. Packer says the doctrine of penal substitution "takes us to the very heart of the gospel" (Packer, "What Did the Cross Achieve?"). Australian theologian Rory Shiner defines the doctrine well:

> The idea of penal substitutionary atonement is, as the name suggests, the claim that Christ's death paid a penalty ("penal"). As Christ did not deserve a penalty, he was paying it for others ("substitutionary"). And, the result of Christ's paying this price for others is that we are now forgiven ("atonement"). . . .
>
> But specifically, when we speak of penal substitutionary atonement, we are highlighting the "in our place" aspect of substitution. The penalty was due to us. It fell on Christ. And this is because he stood where we otherwise should have been, and received what we otherwise should have received.
>
> By this means our sins are atoned. Because Christ substituted as our penalty, we are now able to stand before God guiltless. We have no case to answer, no penalty to pay, no punishment to await. This is what is meant by penal substitutionary atonement. ("In My Place")

Jesus is our example. But more importantly, he is our penal substitute.

Submit to Those in Authority Even When You Suffer Unjustly

1 PETER 2:18-20

Peter continues his teaching that Christians should submit to various authorities in life. He knows there are times when submitting is not a problem. Some laws are no burden at all. However, some authorities prove troublesome. Case in point: slaves who are subject to masters who are "cruel" (v. 18), bring "grief" (v. 19), and cause them to "suffer unjustly" (v. 19). Human nature says to fight back and get even. Christ says to submit and know that "this brings favor with God" (v. 20).

Before diving into these verses, we should make a few observations about slavery in general.[3] First, slavery is regulated by God, but it is not ordained by God. Second, slavery is evil in whatever form it has been practiced in human history. Third, slavery has been practiced in various ways in human history. Some people have sold themselves into slavery to live. Fourth, American slavery was race based, with slaves having no rights or independent existence apart from their masters. Fifth, in the New Testament times a slave was sometimes able to purchase his freedom, though this was the exception. Sixth, Paul encouraged slaves to obtain their freedom if possible (1 Cor 7:17-24). Seventh, Christianity transformed the relationship of master-slave to brother-brother (Philemon). Eighth, Christianity sows the seeds for the destruction of human chattel slavery. Finally, although Peter addresses the master-slave relationship in 1 Peter 2:18-21, these verses readily apply to many of our relationships in the twenty-first century. The world finds these principles nonsense, but the Bible says they invite "favor with God" (vv. 19,20) and follow in the footsteps of Jesus (v. 21).

Do Good to Those Who Treat You Well (2:18)

Peter admonishes, "Household slaves, submit to your masters with all reverence ["respect" ESV] not only to the good and gentle ones but also to the cruel." The initiative lies with slaves. This command may hint that saved slaves were under the authority of unsaved masters. Such submission is to be with all reverence toward God because we ultimately "serve the Lord Christ" (Col 3:24).

In God's goodness, some people work or serve under authority that is "good and gentle," those who treat their subordinates with kindness and consideration. When we find ourselves in these situations, we should be grateful to God for his gracious providence.

---

[3] For a longer treatment see Daniel L. Akin and James Merritt, *Exalting Jesus in 1 Corinthians*, Christ-Centered Exposition Commentary (Nashville, TN: Holman, 2023), 151–53.

Do Good to Those Who Treat You Unjustly (2:18-20)

Vaughan and Lea remind us, "Reverence for God should indeed govern all our conduct" (*1, 2 Peter*, 64). Reverence is needed when we find ourselves in unfair, harsh, and unjust circumstances. When you find yourself serving under a cruel and unjust master or boss, submit. Why? It brings favor with God when you do so "because of a consciousness of God" ("when, mindful of God" ESV). We trust God when we endure grief from suffering unjustly (v. 20). We believe that "the Judge of the whole earth [will] do what is just" (Gen 18:25). Our relationship with God and our obedience to God will be rewarded ("brings favor," vv. 19,20) by God.

Peter tells us in verse 20 to weigh the "spiritual logic" of the situation by asking a rhetorical question: "For what credit is there if when you do wrong and are beaten, you endure it?" Peter asks the question; the answer is obvious: None. If we sin or act unjustly, there is no credit when we suffer. It is what we deserve. In contrast, Peter writes, "But when you do what is good and suffer, if you endure it, this brings favor with God." When we are insulted, mocked, slandered (v. 12), and passed over because we follow Christ, we do what is right. When we are rejected, face false accusations, and suffer, we do what is good and godly. We do not fight back, nor do we seek revenge. We listen to the wisdom of Paul in Romans 12:19-20:

> *Friends, do not avenge yourselves; instead, leave room for God's wrath, because it is written, Vengeance belongs to me; I will repay, says the Lord. But if your enemy is hungry, feed him. If he is thirsty, give him something to drink. For in so doing you will be heaping fiery coals on his head.*

When we suffer the wrong, we follow Christ our "example" and "follow in his steps" (1 Pet 2:21). This is the main emphasis in verses 21-25.

Follow the Example of Jesus When You Suffer Unjustly

1 PETER 2:21-25

Mark Dever writes that the life of Jesus is unique and exemplary (Dever and Lawrence, *It Is Well*, 195). Dever is right. Because Christ's life is unique and exemplary, he can meet us where we are and take us where we need to go, returning us "to the Shepherd and Overseer of [our] souls" (2:25). Peter expounds on three truths related to this wonderful Savior. Isaiah 53 and the Suffering Servant song are foundational to all that Peter writes.

Christ Suffered for Us (2:21-23)

Peter once more applies spiritual logic for his readers. "For you were called to this" (v. 21) refers back to verses 18-20 and the subject of suffering. We were called to suffer unjustly "because Christ also suffered for you, leaving you an example, that you should follow in his steps." Christ suffered "for you," in your place. He is our substitute, which is explained in verse 24. Schreiner writes, "The phrase Christ 'suffered for you' . . . refers to the vicarious sacrifice of Christ, especially since such an idea is explicitly taught in v. 24 and is clearly taught in 3:18" (*1, 2 Peter*, 142). The vicarious sufferings of Christ also have an exemplary aspect. He has left us "an example, that [we] should follow in his steps" (v. 21). Dever notes,

> The word for "example" here conjures up the image or a pattern that taught children how to write correctly, tracing the shape of letters over models or examples. That's what Jesus' life is for the Christian. It is a life that we are to follow in order that we might learn to live a truly, fully human life. (Dever and Lawrence, *It Is Well*, 201)

J. N. D. Kelly says the word "has the air of the schoolroom clinging to it" (*A Commentary*, 120).

Now, spiritual logic demands that we ask, Why should we follow the example of Christ? Why not follow the example of Buddha? Socrates? Ghandi? Mother Teresa? Drawing from Isaiah 53, Peter provides the answer in verses 22-23.

- He did not commit sin.
- No deceit was found in his mouth (Isa 53:9).
- When he was insulted, he did not insult in return (Isa 53:7).
- When he suffered, he did not threaten.
- He entrusted himself to the one who judges justly.

No lie was ever found in the mouth of Jesus. Not once did he retaliate against those who insulted, beat, and crucified him. He prayed for them (Luke 23:24)! Though he could have called on his Father to send twelve legions of angels and wipe out his enemies (Matt 26:53), he did not threaten. Instead, he entrusted ("continued entrusting" ESV) himself to his Father, "who judges justly."

These amazing truths flow from the fact that "he did not commit sin." He is a sinless Savior. He never committed sin! The witness to our Lord's sinlessness finds a mountain of evidence in the Bible. It is a non-negotiable doctrine of the Christian faith.

- Judas called him innocent (Matt 27:41).
- Pilate called him innocent (John 18:38).
- Jesus spoke of his sinlessness (John 8:29).
- Paul said he was sinless (2 Cor 5:21).
- The author of Hebrews said he was sinless (Heb 4:15).
- John said he was sinless (1 John 3:5).
- Peter said he was sinless (1 Pet 2:22).

John and Peter followed and watched Jesus over a number of years. That adds additional weight to their witness to his sinlessness. To err is *not* human. Jesus makes that clear in his sinless life, in his suffering for us, and in the example he provides for us.

Christ Was a Substitute for Us (2:24)

This is one of the great atonement verses in the Bible. Peter draws from Isaiah 53 and Deuteronomy 21:23. We, as sinners, cannot atone for our sins. Only the sinless Savior can do that. Peter writes, "He himself bore our sins in his body." Jesus lived the life we should have lived. He died the death we should have died. He bore in his body the wrath we should have borne. This is sacrificial language. This is substitution language. This is satisfaction language. Jesus, by his death on the cross, took our place, took on the curse of a criminal by his death on the tree (Deut 21:23), and took on the wrath of God. He satisfied the righteous judgment of God.

> Bearing shame and scoffing rude,
> In my place condemned He stood,
> Sealed my pardon with His blood;
> Hallelujah, what a Savior!
> ("Hallelujah, What a Savior!" *Baptist Hymnal*, 242)

Christ died to forgive our sins, but he also died to sins, "so that, having died to sins, we might live for righteousness. By his wounds you have been healed" (v. 24). Because of his work on the cross and our union with Christ, we have died to sins. We continue to die to sin. We have the power to "live a new kind of life" (Schreiner, *1, 2 Peter*, 146). Our new life is not characterized by sin but by righteousness, a God kind of life. Returning to Isaiah 53:5, Peter declares, "By his wounds you have been healed." The death of Christ ("his wounds") is our physical healing ultimately and our spiritual healing immediately. We can sum up the atoning work of Christ like this:

Jesus Christ, the Son of God, by offering himself as a **sacrifice**, by **substituting** himself in our place, paying the penalty of our sin in full by his bloody death and bearing the punishment that should have been ours, **satisfied** the Father's righteous demands, effected a reconciliation between God and man, and became our **justification** by imputing his righteousness to us by faith in his perfect and healing work of atonement.

Christ Is a Shepherd to Us (2:25)

Verse 25 once again takes us back to Isaiah 53, in particular verse 6: "We all went away like sheep; we have all turned to our own way; and the LORD has punished him for the iniquity of us all." We were like lost wandering sheep. But then our Shepherd stepped in to rescue us. He has turned us and returned us. He has taken us to a place of salvation, safety, and security. Our souls now rest in the care of the Good Shepherd and Overseer of our souls. Christ now has absolute authority in our lives as our protector, provider, and pastor. There is no better place to be. There is no better person to whom we can flee.

Conclusion

In 2013, The Presbyterian Church (U.S.A) was revising their hymnal. The much-loved Christian hymn "In Christ Alone" did not make the cut. The Presbyterian Committee on Congregational Song wanted to edit out the phrase "the wrath of God was satisfied." Instead of singing, "'Til on that cross as Jesus died The wrath of God was satisfied," they wanted to substitute the phrase, "the love of God was magnified." The committee opined that the problem was not the word *wrath* but the word *satisfied*. Rev. Chris Joiner said, "But the words of the song don't work. That lyric comes close to saying God killed Jesus. The cross is not an instrument of God's wrath" (Smietana, "Presbyterians' Decision").

Authors Stuart Townend and Keith Getty said no to the change. The committee voted to drop the hymn.

Now, let's be clear. When on the cross as Jesus died, the love of God *was* magnified. Why was it magnified? Because the wrath of God was satisfied. When the Son of God died on the cross and "the LORD [his Father] was pleased to crush him severely" (Isa 53:10), the wrath of God was poured out on his Son and his justice satisfied. The Son of God took our place (substitution) and paid in full our penalty (penal).

The atonement is "perhaps better sung than said" (Shiner, "In My Place"). There is wisdom in that thought. Let us close by drawing from the hymn "When Peace like a River" by Horatio Spafford.

> My sin—oh, the bliss of this glorious thought:
> My sin—not in part but the whole
> Is nailed to the cross and I bear it no more,
> Praise the Lord, praise the Lord, O my soul!
> (*Baptist Hymnal*, 447)

Reflect and Discuss

1. Why must you believe that Jesus paid your penalty?
2. Why should Exodus 21:16 and 1 Timothy 1:10 have prevented American Christians from endorsing the slave trade? What other passages should Christians have paid attention to?
3. What actions is Peter encouraging slaves to avoid during suffering?
4. How do Christians gain favor by suffering unjustly?
5. What promises can encourage Christians when they suffer?
6. What do Christians believe God will do when they suffer? How did God prove his trustworthiness in Jesus?
7. How do verses 22-23 explain what it means to submit with "all reverence"?
8. How can believers evangelize with the hope of a God who judges justly?
9. How is 1 Peter 2:24 a summary of the Christian faith?
10. What is the dominant metaphor you use to think about the need for the gospel (e.g., *rebels* against a *king*; people *walking* in *darkness*; *prodigal son* running from his *father*)? How does the straying-sheep metaphor help you understand the gospel?

The Blessings and Challenges of Marriage

1 PETER 3:1-7

Main Idea: Husbands and wives please God by honoring and being gentle with each other.

I. Wives Should Submit to Their Husbands (3:1-6).
   A. Live with evangelistic wisdom (3:1-2).
   B. Live with beauty that is internal more than external (3:3-4).
   C. Live with worthy role models as your example (3:5-6).

II. Husbands Should Understand Their Wives (3:7).
   A. Grow in your knowledge of them personally.
   B. Grow in your knowledge of them physically.
   C. Grow in your knowledge of them spiritually.

Marriage is one of God's great gifts to us. In Genesis 2 God created the first marriage between a man and a woman, between Adam and Eve. There God tells us, "It is not good for the man to be alone. I will make a helper corresponding to him" (Gen 2:18). God would then make a woman, and he would unite the man and woman in a covenant relationship as the two "become one flesh" (Gen 2:24). Marriage between a man and a woman is a wonderful gift from our great God. It has only one problem: it involves two sinners living with each other. In our fallen world, that is a formula for sparks to fly. Further, imagine one is a Christian and one is not; one is devoted to Jesus and one is not. This difference compounds the challenges and potential for problems. In such situations, what are we to do? Peter, under God's Holy Spirit, provides words of guidance to help us navigate these turbulent waters. He has words of counsel for the wife and the husband.

Wives Should Submit to Their Husbands

1 PETER 3:1-6

Peter began addressing the subject of submission in 1 Peter 2:13. First, he addresses our responsibilities to the government (2:13-17). Second, he addresses how slaves relate to their masters (2:18-25). Now, he addresses how wives and husbands should interact with each other (3:1-7). In each relationship he speaks to those in a subordinate position, to those who have less power and are more vulnerable. The power dynamics may be even more acute in the situation Peter addresses here: it is a saved wife married to a lost husband. What should she do? What should she say? How should she act? Peter's counsel is consistent with what he wrote in 1 Peter 2:13-25. Follow the example of Jesus (2:21) and be submissive (3:1). Wives, yield in your will to the direction and leadership of your husband, even if he is not a follower of Jesus. Note, "voluntary submission is in view here" (Schreiner, *1, 2 Peter*, 148). This is something she willingly chooses to do. The reasons a wife should submit are detailed in verses 1-6.

Live with Evangelistic Wisdom (3:1-2)

"In the same way" is probably not the best translation. It could give the idea that a wife is to submit to her husband the same way a slave submits to his master. The Greek word here functions as a connective to what Peter has just written, and therefore "next" or the ESV's "likewise" serves us better. A wife submits but not like a slave. Further, the exhortation is specific. It is "wives . . . to your own husbands." All women do not submit to all men. The Bible knows nothing of that kind of idea.

The wife in view has a unique challenge. Her husband is among those who "disobey the word." He is lost. He is not a Christian. How should she respond? Should she leave him? Preach to him? No, she should submit so that her husband "may be won over without a word" by the way his wife lives, by his observing her pure, reverent life (vv. 1-2). Her husband will not be won to Christ by nagging or a verbal barrage of Bible verses. He may be won while seeing a transformed life.

He must hear and know the gospel in order to be saved. But that gospel comes wrapped in the package of a beautiful life that is pure, reverent, inwardly attractive, adorned with a gentle and quiet spirit that is of "great worth in God's sight" (v. 4), and evangelistically persuasive in the eyes of her husband. This woman, because she honors Jesus and loves her husband, becomes a master of knowing how to say the right thing, in the right way, at the right time, and for the right reason. Warren Wiersbe says,

> An unsaved husband will not be converted by preaching or nagging in the home. The phrase "without the word" does

> not mean "without the Word of God," because salvation comes through the Word (John 5:24). It means "without talk, without a lot of speaking." Christian wives who preach at their husbands only drive them further from the Lord. . . . It is the character and conduct of the wife that will win the lost husband—not arguments, but such attitudes as submission, understanding, love, kindness, and patience. These qualities are not manufactured; they are the fruit of the Spirit [Gal 5:22-23]. (*Be Hopeful*, 70)

Believers with unbelieving spouses must live so that every moment points their spouses to the gospel.

Live with Beauty That Is Internal More Than External (3:3-4)

In an article titled "Fueled by Social Media, Gen Zer's and Millennials Admit to Overspending on Beauty Products," Maggie Davis notes that "beauty is pain" and "vanity comes at a price" (Davis, "Fueled by Social Media"). Consumers spend an average of $1,754 a year on beauty products, with younger generations spending between $2,408 and $2,670. "In the US, women and girls spend an average of $545 per year on clothing" (Linder, "Money Spent on Clothes"). With this backdrop, Peter's words in verses 3-4 sound strange:

> *Don't let your beauty consist of outward things like elaborate hairstyles and wearing gold jewelry or fine clothes, but rather what is inside the heart* ["rather, the hidden person of the heart" CSB footnote]—*the imperishable quality of a gentle and quiet spirit, which is of great worth in God's sight.*

Peter's primary, but not exclusive, audience is saved wives who have lost husbands that they want to win to Christ (vv. 1-2). He is not opposed to women looking attractive, especially to their husbands. Song of Songs gives biblical support here. Peter is concerned that a woman may give more attention to her appearance than to her heart. He is concerned that a wife may care more about what she looks like on the outside than who she is on the inside. If a wife desires to win her husband to the gospel, the inner life is most important.

Ostentatious and showy hairstyles, jewelry, and fancy clothes may be evidence of a prideful and idolatrous heart (cf. 1 Tim 2:9-10). Vaughan and Lea are correct: "Peter's words are to be taken as a caution against a distorted sense of values," something men are also suspectable to (*1, 2 Peter*, 74). God is always more interested in our heart (1 Pet 3:4). First Samuel 16:7 reminds us, "Humans do not see what the LORD sees, for humans see what is visible, but the LORD sees the heart." He finds beautiful "the imperishable quality of a gentle and quiet spirit" (v. 4). John Piper says "serene" or "tranquil" captures well what Peter is saying ("The Beauty and Behavior of a Godly Woman"). Perhaps Proverbs 31:30 says it best: "Charm is deceptive and beauty is fleeting, but a woman who fears the LORD will be praised."

Live with Worthy Role Models as Your Example (3:5-6)

We all have heroes, people we look up to and even emulate. Peter has told us in 1 Peter 2:21 that our ultimate example for life and unjust suffering is Jesus. Now, for wives—really all women—he points to the matriarch Sarah and, by implication, Rebekah, Rachel, and Leah. Peter makes a general observation about the women of faith "in the past." Of these women, he says they were "holy women who put their hope in God." Their hope was not in this world. Nor did they put their hope in their husbands, though each of the key matriarchs was blessed with a believing husband. Their hope was in the Lord, so they "adorned themselves" by "submitting to their own husbands" (v. 5). Peter cites Sarah (Heb 11:11), but her example is surprising. He references Genesis 18:12, which is the Lord's promise that Abraham and Sarah will have a child in their old age. There we read, "So she laughed to herself: 'After I am worn out and my lord is old, will I have delight?'" Schreiner writes that the verse

> reflects an off-hand comment by Sarah to the idea that she will become pregnant by Abraham. What Peter found remarkable was that she still referred to him with respect and dignity instead of merely calling him an old man (though she did note his age!). We see from this that even in casual situations Sarah respected Abraham's leadership, revealing thereby that her honor of him was part of the warp and woof of her life. (*1, 2 Peter*, 156)

Peter concludes his instruction to wives by blessing them with these words: "You have become her children when you do what is good and do not fear any intimidation" ("anything that is frightening" ESV). John Piper is right:

> Hope in God drives away fear of man. The daughters of Sarah do not fear anything but displeasing God. . . . They wage war on fear, and they defeat it, with the promises of God. ("Holy Women Who Hoped in God")

Before we move to husbands, here is a final word about submission in marriage for the wives: because your Lord and King is Christ, you are not under obligation to obey and submit to your husband if he asks you to do something unbiblical, unethical, illegal, or immoral. The will of Christ for a wife always trumps the will of a husband.

Submission for a wife does not mean a wife is inferior to her husband (see "coheirs" in v. 7). She is not less spiritual than her husband. She is not to be treated like a servant or doormat. She does not always have to agree with her husband. A woman do not check her brain at the marriage altar (Piper, "What Is Submission in Marriage?"). Submission does not mean wives cannot provide counsel and perspective to their husbands. It does not require wives to subject themselves to physical, psychological, and emotional abuse. The same is true for children. Wives may even separate for a season for the hope and health of their marriage (1 Cor 7:10-11).

Now, we turn our attention to Peter's advice to husbands.

Husbands Should Understand Their Wives

1 PETER 3:7

"In the same way," as in verse 1, has the meaning of "likewise" or "next." Peter is moving to address a new group: husbands (Schreiner, *1, 2 Peter*, 159). Saved husbands are in view here. That they receive only one verse should not cause us to erroneously conclude they need less instruction. The instruction husbands receive is comprehensive, direct, and pointed. The primary point is knowledge and understanding of their wives.

Grow in Your Knowledge of Them Personally

Peter calls husbands to "live with [their] wives in an understanding way." The KJV says, "Dwell with them according to knowledge." Husbands should work at knowing and understanding their wives. Kistemaker says,

> Peter wants the husbands to love their wives in a Christian manner. That is, husbands ought to live with their spouses in

> accordance with Christian knowledge (compare Eph. 5:25-33; Col. 3:19). In their marriage, they should demonstrate the love of Jesus that is revealed in the Scriptures and thus be considerate and understanding. Husbands must love and respect their wives in harmony with God's Word. (*Peter*, 124)

A husband needs to develop a "marital radar system." He needs to send out and receive signals from his wife. It is to be hoped that this radar system will develop and grow over time. Watch her. Listen to her. Study her. Become a student of your wife and work hard to change yourself to love her well. It will honor God and bless you.

Grow in Your Knowledge of Them Physically

Peter says we grow in our understanding of our wives "as with a weaker partner." Weaker here means physically, not intellectually, morally, or in any other category. Karen Jobes writes,

> In the context of 1 Peter, "weaker vessel" is primarily understood as indicating physical weakness relative to men's strength. Therefore, Peter's exhortation indirectly addresses the issue of physical abuse. . . . Peter teaches that men whose authority runs roughshod over their women, even with society's full approval, will not be heard by God [when they pray]. (*1 Peter*, 210)

Jobes's observation remains relevant today. Men in many cultures, because they are bigger and stronger, subject women to all sorts of abuse. Beatings, whippings, and sexual abuse are far too prevalent around the globe. Men who follow Christ have a different perspective and a different ethic. Size and strength allow men to provide, protect, and serve—not to exploit, harm, and abuse. Physical strength is a gift of service from God.

Grow in Your Knowledge of Them Spiritually

Some believe "understanding" in the first part of verse 7 is talking about our understanding of God, his Word, and his teachings on marriage. That is certainly possible, but here in the last part of verse 7 there is no doubt. As we live in an understanding way, caring for our wives as a unique and precious vessel, we will "show them honor" because we recognize their equal value and worth to our Savior as "coheirs of the grace of life." Piper writes,

> Men, let this sink in and dwell on it long and hard. Fellow heir, so heir comes from the inheritance back in 1 Peter 1. We are born again to a living hope, to an inheritance, undefiled, unfading, imperishable kept in heaven for you, and she's got the same one.
>
> She's going to be a queen of the universe someday. You sleep with a queen. You sleep with an heiress of the world. That's not an exaggeration. You sleep with an heiress of the world, the earth. That should have an effect on you in terms of kindness, respect, tenderness, listening, marveling at what you have in this house. We are not amazed enough at the marvel of who we are. Representing Christ, representing the church, fellow heir the grace of life. We don't marvel enough at the wonder of our wives or our husbands. ("Men, Love and Lead Your Wives").

Peter closes with an important spiritual observation. If husbands don't work at understanding their wives, treat them well because of the husbands' superior physical strength, and honor them as coheirs of all they have in Jesus, then God will not hear their prayers. The prayers will be "hindered." If a husband is not right with his wife, he cannot be right with God. Pray all you want. The prayers will be impeded, thwarted. They will hit the ceiling and fall back to the floor. Further, husbands living in sin have a hard time praying. No need to go to God just yet. Best to go to your wife first and make things right.

Conclusion

Two Christians in marriage are still two sinners in marriage. This is a challenge and one made more difficult when one mate is lost. Marriage is hard work. But there are ten ways husbands and wives can work to love their spouses and create a God-honoring marriage.

1. **Make a choice (commitment) to love and humbly serve your mate (Phil 2:3-5).** They are made in God's image (Gen 1:26-27) and Christ died for them (John 3:16). Accepting them does not mean you always agree with them or affirm their actions (Acts 5:29).

2. **Receive your mate as someone valuable in your life.** They are God's gift to you as divine, heavenly sandpaper! God will use them to conform you more to the image of his Son (Rom 8:28-30).

3. **Seek to live wisely and accept personal responsibility for your relationship (Prov 14:16; 15:12,32; 28:13; Eph 4:29-31).** Do not play the blame game. Remember, you are a sinner too, and you will also do sinful things.

4. **Rejoice and value the differences, looking for the positive.** God made you different so that you complement each other (Gen 2:18).

5. **Determine to communicate in a godly and positive manner (Prov 4:24; 10:11,19-21,31-32; 26:20-28):**
   a. Share (Prov 11:13-14; 25:11-12; Eph 4:15). Use "I" messages.
   b. Listen to the words and the heart (Prov 12:15; 15:22; 19:27; 21:23; 29:11,20; Jas 1:19). Be quick to listen!
   c. Talk (Prov 15:1,23,28; 16:24; Eph 4:25-27; Jas 1:19). Be slow to speak!

6. **Never assume anything.** Grow in your understanding of your mate (Prov 3:3-4,7; 17:27-28; 18:1-2,13,15; 19:2; 1 Pet 3:7).

7. **Be an encourager (Prov 3:27; 12:25; 15:15; 17:22; 1 Cor 8:1; 13:7).** Look for the positive whenever possible. You attract more bees with honey than with vinegar.

8. **Be honest and willing to admit your own failures.** Learn to say, "I am sorry. I was wrong. Will you forgive me?" (Eph 4:32; Jas 5:16).

9. **Accept yourself in Christ (Gal 2:20; Eph 1:3-14).** It will free you to love and accept your mate without either a superiority or an inferiority complex (1 Cor 13:4).

10. **Learn to be a lover.** Learn to speak in a language that she will understand (1 Cor 13:4-8). If we reflect on the gospel with Gary Chapman's *The 5 Love Languages* in mind, we see how Jesus treated us, and we can follow his example.

- *Words*: Jesus spoke words of love and healing.
- *Touch*: Jesus touched the sick and dead and brought healing and life.
- *Service*: Jesus was the Suffering Servant of the Lord who washed feet and died on the cross for our sins.
- *Gifts*: Jesus gives us the gift of eternal life and so much more.
- *Time*: Jesus is always with us promising never to leave or forsake us.

Reflect and Discuss

1. What have you been taught about submission?
2. How have you seen submission modeled? Have you had good or bad examples of submission?
3. How may a wife view her unbelieving husband differently once she becomes a believer? Why may a believing wife struggle to submit to her nonbelieving husband?
4. Why would a husband believe the gospel because of his wife's pure and reverent life?
5. What is the problem with a beauty that is only outward?
6. How does 1 Peter 3:7 correct faulty ideas about submission?
7. How can the church protect women from abusive husbands?
8. Since a wife is a coheir, how should a husband interact with her?
9. Why must husbands set aside their own preferences in order to serve their wives?
10. What should you think about God, since he refuses to hear the prayers of an uncaring husband?

Live to Be a Blessing because God Is Watching

1 PETER 3:8-12

Main Idea: Believers love one another and bless anyone who harms them.

I. **Know How to Treat Your Brothers and Sisters in Christ (3:8).**
   A. Be like-minded.
   B. Be sympathetic.
   C. Love one another.
   D. Be compassionate.
   E. Be humble.

II. **Know How to Respond to Those Who Treat You Badly (3:9).**
   A. Do not repay evil with evil.
   B. Do not repay insult with insult.
   C. Give a blessing because you will receive a blessing.

III. **Know Who Is Always Watching What You Do (3:10-12).**
   A. God is watching, so show him you love the life he has given you (3:10).
   B. God is watching, so guard your tongue (3:10).
   C. God is watching, so do what is good (3:11).
   D. God is watching, so be a peacemaker and not a troublemaker (3:11).
   E. God is watching, so live righteously and know he hears your prayers (3:12).
   F. God is watching, so remember he opposes the evil (3:12).

In C. S. Lewis's book *The Problem of Pain*, Lewis quotes the great church father Augustine and writes, "God wants to give us something, but cannot because our hands are full—there's nowhere for God to put it" (*The Problem of Pain*, 84). God loves us and wants to give us blessings, the greatest blessing being himself. Unfortunately, our hands are too often full. Sometimes they are full of good things that we have turned into idols. Sometimes they are full of sinful things like divisiveness, hatred, pride, evil, bitterness, a spirit of revenge, or a wicked tongue that is out of control. Peter addresses such sins in 1 Peter 3:8-12. He does not want us to hurt others and ourselves because we are eaten up by anger and bitterness. He wants us to bless others, even our enemies, and to continue to follow the example of Jesus and walk in his footsteps (2:21).

Peter has addressed several groups up to this point. He calls for a spirit of submissiveness in 1 Peter 2:13–3:7. Now, in 3:8-12, he draws his argument to a close. The word "finally" that begins verse 8 tips us off. The phrase "all of you" settles the matter. The whole community, the entire church, is now in view. His admonitions and encouragements are for all of us.

Know How to Treat Your Brothers and Sisters in Christ

1 PETER 3:8

Verse 8 contains five adjectives describing a life that follows the example of Jesus (2:21) and characterizes the life of a Christian. Each is an implied command. Schreiner points out the verse contains a chiasm, which points to a focus on brotherly love:

A – Harmony ["like-minded" CSB]
B – Sympathy
C – Brotherly Love ["love one another" CSB]
B' – Compassion
A' – Humility (*1, 2 Peter*, 163–64)

He notes, "Brotherly love is the middle term, showing that it is the most important of all the virtues and that the other virtues are embraced in the call to love one another as a family" (*1, 2 Peter*, 163–64).

Be Like-Minded

This means to live in harmony, having the same mind (cf. Phil 2:2). Be "united in spirit, aim and purpose" (Vaughan and Lea, *1, 2 Peter*, 81). We are together in mind and mission. We are not divisive, selfish in ambition, vainly conceited, or rupturing the fellowship (Phil 2:3-4).

Be Sympathetic

This means to share in the feelings of others: "Feel what others feel so that you can respond with sensitivity to the need" (Piper, "Your Calling Is to Bless Believers"). We are not hard-hearted, callous, or indifferent to the hurts and needs of others.

Love One Another

This calls for brotherly love (Gk *philadelphos*). We love others like family because they are our brothers and sisters in Christ. We worship the same Father, adore the same Savior, and are indwelled by the same Spirit. Calvin says, "Where God is known as Father, there only brotherhood really exists" ("Commentaries," 102).

Be Compassionate

This ("a tender heart" ESV) points to having deep inward feelings and affections for others. Luther says,

> This word I cannot explain except by giving an illustration. Observe how a mother or father acts towards their child; for example, when a mother sees her child enduring anguish, her whole inward being is moved, and her heart within her body. (*Commentary*, 146)

Luther then points us to the famous story of two women who claimed a baby boy was theirs and were brought before King Solomon to decide the case (1 Kings 3:16-28). When Solomon said, "Cut the living boy in two and give half to one and half to the other" (v. 25), the true mother "felt great compassion" and said, "My lord, give her [the lying woman] the living baby, but please don't have him killed!" (v. 26). Solomon saw who was the true mother and gave the boy to her. Luther says, "We should be heartily kind and motherly, and the heart should be thoroughly penetrated. Such a disposition should one Christian bear toward another" (*Commentary*, 146).

Be Humble

This refers to an attitude of the heart where you esteem others more important than yourself. We are not arrogant, prideful, or self-centered. We are "others focused" in our outlook on life. J. N. D. Kelly says, "Humble-minded expresses a characteristic directly modeled on Christ" (*A Commentary*, 136).

These five characteristics tell us how we should live with one another in the body of Christ. It is an attractive life that should cause the lost to stop, notice, and be drawn to join us. Peter will address that in verse 9.

Know How to Respond to Those Who Treat You Badly

1 PETER 3:9

Pastor Warren Wiersbe wisely writes,

> As Christians, we can live on one of three levels. We can return evil for good, which is the satanic level. We can return good for good and evil for evil, which is the human level. Or, we can return good for evil, which is the divine level. Jesus is the perfect example of this latter approach (1 Peter 2:21-23). As God's loving children, we must do more than give "an eye for an eye, and a tooth for a tooth" (Matt. 5:38-48), which is the basis for *justice*. We must operate on the basis of *mercy*, for that is the way God deals with us. (*Be Hopeful*, 80)

Verse 9 redirects our focus. In verse 8 our attention was on how we treat our brothers and sisters in Christ. Verse 9 places our attention on unbelievers. When we are mistreated by action or word, what should be our response? Peter will again point us to the example of Christ seen in 2:18-23.

Do Not Repay Evil with Evil

Peter tells us to "not pay back evil for evil." *The Message* says, "No retaliation." Peter's words are similar to Paul's in Romans 12:17: "Do not repay anyone evil for evil." Both admonitions find their origin in the teachings of Jesus in the Sermon on the Mount (Matt 5:38-46; Luke 6:27-29). William Brownson captures the radical, countercultural nature of Peter's words:

> "Do not return evil for evil, or reviling for reviling, but on the contrary, bless." There it is again, *that miracle style of life*. With most people, you reap what you sow. Shove them and they will shove back. Sow an insult and you will reap a choicer one. That's the age-old pattern, and it leads to mounting hate and violence. But the Christians whom Peter describes don't feed back what they receive. They don't merely answer in kind. Somehow they transform what comes at them, so that insults generate prayers and hate comes back as love. (*Tried by Fire*, 66; emphasis added)

Do Not Repay Insult with Insult

"Not paying back evil for evil" is a general statement that looks to our actions. Not returning "insult for insult" is a more specific statement that addresses the tongue. It points to the example of our Lord in 1 Peter 2:23. When we are abused by the words of others, we don't repay them with more abusive words. If they cut with their words, we don't cut them back with a sharper blow and a deeper wound. Kistemaker says,

> Peter indicates that the readers are trying to settle injuries and insults on their own terms. He tells them to stop retaliating; repaying evil for evil and insult for insult has no place in the Christian religion. (*Peter*, 128)

A sharp wit and a sharp tongue may impress the world, but it will receive no applause from heaven. It gets no praise from God (Jas 3). Consider the wise prayer of Psalm 141:3: "LORD, set up a guard for my mouth; keep watch at the doors of my lips." Continually remind yourself of this truth: in the spiritual realm the tongue is connected to the heart. The former reveals the content of the latter.

Give a Blessing because You Will Receive a Blessing

The final phrase in verse 9 provides a summary and a motivation for the "miracle style of life" that is to be the pattern of the child of God. We do not repay evil with evil or insult with insult. No, contrary to the natural impulse of our flesh, we give a blessing. By action and word, we demonstrate unconditional love. We seek the best for others, even our enemies. Because of the transforming power of the new birth on the inside (1:3,23), we react supernaturally on the outside. We seek what is best for those who seek what is worst for us. We take delight in this service. Christ calls us to this. Peter Davids provides excellent insight into this new reality, tying our calling to bless others with our new status as holy and royal priests. He writes,

> The word translated "blessing" meant in secular Greek simply "to speak good of a person," but in the NT, because of the use of the Greek term in the Greek translation of the OT, the word means "bless." Blessing was seen as something that really brought good to the person blessed. God, of course, is the chief blesser (e.g., Gen. 12:2; 26:3; 49:25), but patriarchs (e.g.,

> Gen. 27:4,33) and especially priests (Num. 6:22-26; Sir. 50:20-21) blessed. In Peter it is natural that all Christians should bless, for he has already recognized them all as priests (2:9). This is a concrete way of forgiving offending persons and doing good to them, just as God does. (*First Epistle of Peter*, 126)

Our motivation for being a blessing to others is twofold. First, we "were called for this." As our Lord has blessed us abundantly and overflowingly, he calls us to follow in his steps and bless others. However, we are not saved by blessing others; we bless others because we are saved. Second, Jesus said, "Blessed are the merciful, for they will be shown mercy" (Matt 5:7). We bless others for a moment, but our heavenly Father blesses us forever. Future blessings guide us to bless others in the present. Future hope matters for life now.

Know Who Is Always Watching What You Do

1 PETER 3:10-12

Peter grounds his closing argument in the Christian Scriptures of his day, our Old Testament. His text is a psalm of David, Psalm 34:12-16. The entire psalm speaks of the Lord's deliverance and salvation for those who "taste and see that the LORD is good" (Ps 34:8; 1 Pet 2:3). E. Y. Mullins (1860–1928) said Psalm 34 is "an ancient recipe for a happy life" (quoted in Vaughan and Lea, *1, 2 Peter*, 82). Psalm 34 also addresses fears (v. 4), the poor person (v. 6), troubles (v. 6), the brokenhearted (v. 18), and afflictions (vv. 19,21), making the psalm relevant for the sufferings and trials being endured by Peter's audience. Psalm 34:20 applies to the crucifixion of Jesus in John 19:31-33. Peter highlights six truths for our action and meditation.

God Is Watching, so Show Him You Love the Life He Has Given You (3:10)

The word "for" connects verses 8-9 to verses 10-12. The "life" and "good days" of this verse include this present life and the life to come. It includes "the entire existence of the Christian with the Creator, both the temporal present and the eschatological future . . . [our] inheritance" (Jobes, *1 Peter*, 224). "To love life and to see good days" is an example of Hebrew parallelism. Lenski says, "David and Peter are not thinking of easy, pleasant, sunny days but of a life and of days that are full of rich fruit" (*Interpretation,* 144). In other words, we demonstrate by our obedience and transformed lives a passion for life now and the life to come. As an act of faith, we say to God, "I trust you have the best for me." Experiencing evil and reviling is intended by God to bring a better life and good days ahead. Our God is using them to conform us to the image of his Son (Rom 8:29). Christlike responses give evidence of faith and trust in my Lord's purposes and plans.

God Is Watching, so Guard Your Tongue (3:10)

"Let him keep his tongue from evil and his lips from speaking deceit." The first phrase is general. The second phrase specifies lying. Because we want to love life and see good days, we will allow that hope to keep our tongues from evil. Hope will guard us from saying the wrong thing in the wrong way and for the wrong reasons. This admonition looks back to 1 Peter 2:1 and 3:9. If Peter repeatedly addresses problems with the tongue, it must mean there were problems in these communities with the tongue. Suffering and trials can make a harsh or deceitful tongue appealing. These are times we need to trust our God and seek the assistance of his Holy Spirit (Gal 5:22-23).

God Is Watching, so Do What Is Good (3:11)

The word "evil" occurs five times in this passage (v. 9 twice, 10,11,12), a passage that is addressed to the church. That should cause all of us to pause. David (Ps 34) and Peter call God's people to a basic posture. "Let him turn away from evil and do what is good." This is a call to action. Living a good life that reflects the gospel is not a life of passivity. It is a life that loves God, knows his Word, and pursues what pleases him. It contrasts with a life that is indifferent to God, ignorant of God's Word, and uninterested in what pleases God. At bottom, we are to love what God loves and hate what God hates.

God Is Watching, so Be a Peacemaker and Not a Troublemaker (3:11)

Jesus said in Matthew 5:9, "Blessed are the peacemakers, for they will be called sons of God." One way to turn from evil and do what is good is to "seek peace and pursue it." Schreiner is right:

> Peace can easily be disrupted, especially when others mistreat and even abuse us. . . . Such peace will only be preserved if believers do not insult and revile others, if they extend forgiveness to those who injure them. (*1, 2 Peter*, 167)

Paul would add, "But if you bite and devour one another, watch out, or you will be consumed by one another" (Gal 5:15). Troublemakers do not have bright futures. In time, they cannibalize themselves.

God Is Watching, so Live Righteously and Know God Hears Your Prayers (3:12)

We have a God who sees and hears. He is attentive to the righteous when they suffer trials. Evil persons come against us, but God sees what's happening. Evil people cause us to suffer, but God hears our prayers. We are his sons and daughters whom he redeemed with the blood of his Son (1:19; 2:24). Banish the thought that he is unaware of or unconcerned with your plight. Calvin rightly reminds us,

> It ought to be a consolation to us, sufficient to mitigate all evils, that we are looked upon by the Lord, so that he will bring us help in due time . . . for were not the Lord to care for his people, they would be like sheep exposed to wolves. ("Commentaries," 104)

God Is Watching, so Remember He Opposes the Evil (3:12)

The last phrase of verse 12 is the antithesis of the first phrase. God's eyes see the righteous, and his ears hear their call. In contrast "the face of the Lord is against those who do what is evil." Evil people will miss out on the Lord's blessings in this life. Even worse than this, they will miss out on his blessings in eternity. Tragically, no inheritance is kept for them in heaven (1:4). God takes his stand against them, and there is nothing bright or hopeful about their future. Luther captures well the disposition of our God for those who mock his ways, count him unworthy of worship, and hatefully mistreat his children:

> For Peter says further that the face of the Lord is upon them that do evil; he does not behold them with a friendly eye, as he does the righteous, but with an angry countenance. In a person

> who is very angry one sees how his whole countenance is disfigured and changed; he looks sour, bites his teeth, wrinkles his brow, mouth and nose, and in general looks like one who will knock things to pieces with all his might. With such a countenance, Peter says, the Lord beholds those who do evil, so that he will utterly root out their memory from the earth, as all historians testify that he has rooted out many great and mighty potentates, that neither a branch nor a root of them remains. So the final result is that all who persecute the righteous do themselves only harm, lose the blessing and the friendly countenance of the Lord, will not only be uprooted here in time, but will also still possess their guilt yonder; therefore they must be condemned forever. (*Commentary*, 155)

Conclusion

Luther was known for his fiery temper, salty language, and opposition to Roman Catholicism that strangled the church. However, he should also be known for his love for souls. As he reflected on the lost and the evils they often inflict upon God's people, he was moved to pray for their salvation and their good.

> Beloved Father, since our adversaries have so horribly fallen in thy wrath and have cast themselves so lamentably into eternal fire, I pray thou wouldst forgive them, rescue them from thy anger and show them grace, just as thou hast done to me. For, as I said, just as he looks upon the righteous with grace, so he frowns upon the wicked, wrinkles his countenance and in anger turns upon them. Since we therefore know that he looks upon us graciously and upon them ungraciously, we should have mercy and pity upon them, and pray that God would increase our faith to believe that his face is friendly toward us who suffer, and then be cheerful and give understanding to those who persecute us, so that they may believe that God is angry with them, and that they may be terrified and converted. (*Commentary*, 155–56)

May his heart become ours.

Reflect and Discuss

1. Why do believers need reminding to work for each other's good? Are believers capable of doing evil if they have the Holy Spirit?
2. Why does it matter that believers think and feel differently about one another?
3. What will believers do if they think and feel contrary to 1 Peter 2:8?
4. What are obvious and subtle ways people can repay evil for evil? Can believers disguise paying evil for evil as righteous?
5. How is blessing a more powerful weapon against evil?
6. What must a Christian believe about God in order to bless those who harm them?
7. How do "good days" come from living righteously?
8. How does the theme of words unite this chapter? Why can words create love, humility, or evil?
9. What motives cause someone to be deceitful?
10. What consequences come when God's face is against someone?

Make a Case for Your Faith

1 PETER 3:13-17

Main Idea: Suffering Christians testify about God by their good conduct and hope in Christ.

I. Be Ready for Action.

II. Be Zealous for What Is Right (3:13-14).

A. Realize you may suffer (3:14).

B. Fear God, not people (3:14).

III. Be Prepared with a Defense (3:15).

A. Honor Christ as Lord in your heart.

B. Be able to give a well-defended hope.

IV. Be Active in Doing Good (3:16-17).

A. Be gracious in attitude (3:16).

B. Cultivate a clear conscience (3:16).

C. Be known for good behavior (3:17).

D. Trust in the will of God no matter what (3:17).

In 2011, United Methodist Pastor Martin Thielen wrote a so-called Christian apologetic titled *What's the Least I Can Believe and Still Be a Christian? A Guide to What Matters Most.* He attempts to "confront fundamentalists with 10 things Christians don't need to believe." In the table of contents (vii–viii) he lists,

1. God Causes Cancer, Car Wrecks, and Other Catastrophes
2. Good Christians Don't Doubt
3. True Christians Can't Believe in Evolution
4. Women Can't Be Preachers and Must Submit to Men
5. God Cares about Saving Souls but Not about Saving Trees
6. Bad People Will Be "Left Behind" and Then Fry in Hell
7. Jews Won't Make It to Heaven
8. Everything in the Bible Should Be Taken Literally
9. God Loves Straight People but Not Gay People
10. It's OK for Christians to Be Judgmental and Obnoxious

Thielen believes he is presenting a twenty-first-century version of Christianity that provides "a compelling faith story to tell" (*What's the Least*, 159). He believes he is presenting a necessary alternative that will solve problems in people's views about Christianity. However, what he provides is a false caricature of historic, evangelical Christianity and a false and inaccurate portrayal of biblical truth. The book does not defend true Christianity. It distorts true Christianity.

Yet, we should not dismiss his thesis too quickly. Christians are often their own worst enemy. Further, non-Christians often view Christians in a negative light because they are offended by them, not their gospel. When we make a case for our faith in the twenty-first century, we must speak the truth in love (Eph 4:15). Like Jesus, we need to be full of grace and truth (John 1:14).

A helpful and faithful approach to apologetics, to making a case for your faith, is found in 1 Peter 3:13-18. The apostle Peter knew that Christians would face the challenge "to give a defense [Gk *apologia*] . . . for the hope that is in you" (v. 15). He knew we *must* be able to explain and defend *what* we believe and *why* we believe. Our assignment is not new. The circumstances and context may change, but Christians have been defending the faith since the first century against those *outside* and *inside* the church. We will continue to do so until Christ comes again.

Peter challenges Christians who were facing opposition and suffering to be good apologists. He wants them to be prepared defenders of the faith. He provides a threefold strategy that applies any place and at any time. It is indeed a divinely inspired strategy for how to make a case for our faith.

Be Ready for Action

Peter has challenged us to be like-minded, sympathetic, loving, compassionate, and humble (v. 8). He says not to pay back "evil for evil or insult for insult." Instead, we should bless those who treat us badly and insult us (v. 9). Why? Because we were called to this when we came to Jesus and because we will be blessed by God. He continues by citing Psalm 34:12-16, telling us to guard our tongues (v. 10) and to do good (v. 11) because the Lord sees it all. He hears our prayers when we tell him what is going on (v. 12). Further, "the face of the Lord is against those who do what is evil." God is on our side, and he is with us no matter what.

With such divine preparation and promise, we are now ready for action in defending our faith.

Be Zealous for What Is Right

1 PETER 3:13-14

Peter begins with a rhetorical question: "Who then will harm you if you are devoted to what is good?" Answer: no one! Like Paul says in Romans 8:31, "If God is for us, who is against us?" (Schreiner, *1, 2 Peter*, 170).

We hold the truth with conviction and humility. We pursue what is right with firmness and grace. We do what is right and in the right way. Vaughan and Lea put it, "When believers are wholeheartedly devoted to the good they are beyond the reach of 'harm' but not beyond the reach of suffering" (*1, 2 Peter*, 86).

Realize You May Suffer (3:14)

Peter does not want us to misunderstand. Suffering for the gospel and the truth is always a possibility. Verse 14 makes this clear. In a secularized culture or an environment hostile to Christianity, you may "suffer for righteousness." You may be called narrow-minded, a religious bigot, a closed-minded fundamentalist, a neanderthal. It is even possible you could lose your job, be denied a promotion, have friendships come to an end, and be cut off from family. You may suffer physical persecution. You may die for King Jesus (see Luke 21:16-19). Many brothers and sisters around the world are suffering. Yet, we must realize there is good in it. "You are blessed." Suffering provides an opportunity to learn what it means to be true disciples of Jesus. Jesus said in Matthew 5:10-12,

> *Blessed are those who are persecuted because of righteousness, for the kingdom of heaven is theirs. You are blessed when they insult you and persecute you and falsely say every kind of evil against you because of me. Be glad and rejoice, because your reward is great in heaven. For this is how they persecuted the prophets who were before you.*

Peter Davids is right: "Some people are so twisted that they will persecute a person just because he or she is righteous, for that righteousness infuriates them" (*First Epistle of Peter*, 130). However, be encouraged! God sees. God knows. He will bless, if not in this life, then in the life to come (see 5:10).

Fear God, Not People (3:14).

All of us fear someone or something. To deny this is to be dishonest with ourselves. We should have fear. The key is knowing whom to fear (Luke 12:5)! Peter says concerning those who may persecute us, "Do not fear them or be intimidated ["troubled" ESV]." *The Message* paraphrases it, "Don't give the opposition a second thought." Why? Because you fear God more than you fear man!

Peter's words are not some superficial pep talk or pregame motivational speech. It is a profound and deeply meaningful alternative to how so many live today. We fear God more than people. We fear what God can do more than what people can do to us. We determine to follow a simple but basic conviction all our life: all that matters in life is that we please God. We trust our Savior and believe he has a purpose in our suffering. We believe it is for our good and for his glory (Rom 8:28).

Be Prepared with a Defense

1 PETER 3:15

John Piper helps us see the close connection between verse 14 and verse 15 when he writes,

> So put your hope in his promise (v. 14a) [that you will be blessed], be fearless before men (v. 14b), and the result will be that you will sanctify Christ as Lord in your heart—you will show that Christ is valuable above all this world. Hallow him by hoping in him—fearlessly. ("Christ Is Hallowed in Us When We Hope in Him")

With spiritual, godly, and personal readiness and preparation, we will be able to bear a faithful witness to those we meet. We will be ready to share with clarity and conviction the gospel of Jesus Christ that, as 1 Peter 1:3 says, "has given us new birth into a living hope through the resurrection of Jesus Christ from the dead."

Honor Christ as Lord in Your Heart

There is a right way and a wrong way to make a case for your faith. The right way:

- "In your hearts regard Christ the Lord as holy" (CSB).
- "In your hearts revere Christ as Lord" (NIV).
- "Sanctify Christ as Lord in your hearts" (NASB).
- "In your hearts honor Christ the Lord as holy" (ESV).
- "Keep your hearts at attention, in adoration before Christ, your Master" (*The Message*).

Honoring Christ as Lord in our life means honoring him as God and King in our life. We do not honor someone or something else. It is, as Paul says in Colossians 1:18, seeing "that he might come to have first place in everything." Honor Christ as Lord in your hearts, and you will slay the idols of the heart. Honor Christ as Lord in your hearts, and you will not fear people but hope in him. Honor Christ as Lord in your heart, and you will always be ready to make a case for your faith. Peter is grounding his argument in Isaiah 8:12-13, where the prophet said, "Do not fear what they fear; do not be terrified. You are to regard only the LORD of Armies as holy. Only he should be feared; only he should be held in awe." Context is critical. Always regard displeasing God as more fearful and dreadful than displeasing any person. "Regard him [Christ] as unique, one of a kind, without peer or rival in purity, rectitude and goodness" (Piper, "Christ Is Hallowed in Us When We Hope in Him").

To fear people is to doubt and distrust Christ. Since unbelief is what displeases him most, honoring him as Lord and as holy means trusting him and his promises with all our heart, no matter what. Charles Spurgeon says,

> God is too wise to err, too good to be unkind; leave off doubting him, and begin to trust him, for in so doing, thou wilt put a crown on his head, but in doubting him thou dost trample his crown beneath thy feet. ("Fear Not," 396)

Be Able to Give a Well-Defended Hope

Making a case for your faith means being "ready at any time to give a defense [Gk *pros apologia*, "provide an apologetic"] to anyone who asks you for a reason for the hope that is in you" (v. 15). You do not have to be a scholar to give a defense of your hope. First Peter was written for common people, many of whom were illiterate. The key to giving a compelling apologetic is the person and work of Christ on our behalf. Verse 18 speaks to this:

> *For Christ also suffered for sins once for all, the righteous for the unrighteous, that he might bring you to God. He was put to death in the flesh but made alive by the Spirit.*

Listen again to how Piper puts it. This quotation is lengthy, but I cannot improve on it:

> The reason we aren't more free and natural in testifying to our neighbors and associates about the reality of our hope in Christ is that we don't feel very hopeful. And if our hearts are not full of hope in the promises of Christ, then here is what happens when an occasion arrives to make a case for our hope: we sense it as a duty to defend doctrine instead of a delight to tell somebody why we are so hopeful. I saw, like I had never seen before, that witnessing will always be a burdensome duty to defend a doctrine as long as Christianity means for us simply accepting certain doctrines as true and keeping a certain list of do's and don'ts. So many people in the church have simply inherited the motions of church life and outward morality and piety, but the heartfelt reality of Christ and joyful hope in his promises are foreign to their experience. Such people can always make a case for doctrine, but they cannot make a case for the hope within them, because they don't feel any hope brimming up within their hearts.
>
> What this means, then, just as the text says, is that the way to get ready to make a case for your hope is to get hopeful. That is what was so exciting. It simplified matters. Don't meditate beforehand on how to answer somebody else's questions. Apply yourself to settling the questions of your own heart. We have to find for ourselves reason enough to get over our fear of men and have a lively hope. If our own hope does not spring from something Christ did and said, then it is a mere sham to try to make a case for anyone else to hope in Christ. But if we search out the promises of Christ and meditate on his character and work for the sake of banishing our own fear and kindling our own hope, then this very act of

> reverencing Christ for ourselves will be the best preparation for making a case for our hope to others. . . .
>
> [S]o then our primary activity in preparing to witness is to keep our own hearts happy in God. Morning by morning we have to go to the Word, not to anxiously amass arguments for every possible rebuttal somebody might have. . . . No, we go to the Word because we are so desperately needy, our own hope wanes. We have fears that need to be overcome by the promises of God. We have doubts that need to be answered. The fight of faith is waged on our knees with the sword of the Spirit, the Word of God, and prayer. And when we emerge from that encounter with God with a renewed and lively hope in his promises, we will be ready to make a case for our hope. For God only calls us to tell others the reasons which that very day are making us hopeful in Christ. ("Make a Case for Your Hope")

Why do we hope in Christ above all else? Why do we love him and treasure him above all else? Our answer may be grounded in the incomparable greatness of his person and work. As Charles Wesley wrote, "Amazing love! How can it be that Thou, my God, should die for me?" ("And Can It Be," *Baptist Hymnal*, 250). Our answer may have to do with the Bible's divine inspiration and the trustworthiness of eyewitness authors in the New Testament. It may come from the evidence of fulfilled prophecy, the empty tomb, the resurrection, the power of changed lives, and that the grand redemptive story of the Bible (creation → fall → redemption → new creation) makes sense of the world. Add to all of this the insight of Blaise Pascal (1623–1662), the brilliant Christian French mathematician, physicist, inventor, writer, and philosopher who said in *Pensées* 423, "The heart has its reasons which reason knows nothing of," and you are on the way to "always being prepared to make a defense to anyone who asks you for a reason for the hope that is in you."[4] In other words, it is one thing to know Jesus as an object of

---

[4] Do not misunderstand Pascal's meaning. Peter Kreeft correctly writes, "This, the most famous of Pascal's sayings . . . is *not* sentimentalism or irrationalism. Pascal does not oppose the heart to reason or demean reason by exalting the heart. On the contrary, he says the heart has its *reasons*. The heart does not only feel, it sees. The heart has an eye in it" (*Christianity*, 231–32; emphases original).

scholarly interest and popular perception. It is altogether different to know him as the lover of our souls.

C. S. Lewis said it so well:

> If I find in myself a desire which no experience in this world can satisfy, the most probable explanation is that I was made for another world. If none of my earthly pleasures satisfy it, that does not prove that the universe is a fraud. Probably earthly pleasures were never meant to satisfy it, but only to arouse it, to suggest the real thing. If that is so, I must take care, on the one hand, never to despise, or be unthankful for, these earthly blessings, and on the other, never to mistake them for the something else of which they are only a kind of copy, or echo, or mirage. I must keep alive in myself the desire for my true country, which I shall not find till after death; I must never let it get snowed under or turned aside; I must make it the main object of life to press on to that other country and to help others to do the same. (*Mere Christianity*, 136–37)

Be Active in Doing Good

1 PETER 3:16-17

I often give the following advice when I do premarital counsel: "Strive to do the right thing for the right reason in the right way and at the right time if at all possible." Doing the wrong thing in the wrong way at the wrong time leads to disaster. Doing the right thing in the wrong way at the wrong time leads to resistance. Doing the right thing in the right way at the right time leads to success. Peter knew this when it came to giving a defense. A gracious and wise witness will more likely receive a positive and receptive hearing. Peter closes his argument by providing four basic principles to guide us.

Be Gracious in Attitude (3:16)

When you tell someone why you love Jesus and worship him as your God and King, do it "with gentleness and reverence ["respect" NET]." *The Message* says, "always with the utmost courtesy."

An overbearing personality, a superiority complex, and a know-it-all attitude that is arrogant and rude dishonor Christ, misrepresent the gospel, and will effectively ruin any witness for Christ.

It is never right to be rude. It is never right to disrespect others. Don't misrepresent the love of God. We must love others like we have been loved by Jesus.

Cultivate a Clear Conscience (3:16)

Having a "clear conscience" before God means we are free from guilt and have nothing to hide. We live a transparent life of honesty, truthfulness, and integrity. It is not a perfect life, but it is one that seeks to follow Christ (1 Cor 11:1) and is growing in his likeness as the gospel works itself out in your life.

Such a life will silence those who misrepresent and insult you. It will put to shame those who accuse you and "disparage your good conduct in Christ."

The phrase "in Christ" is important. Our union with Christ is the energizing source and power of the beauty, excellence, and attractiveness of our Christian behavior. Christ alters and transforms the way we think, feel, speak, and act. A clear conscience that leads to "good conduct in Christ" will enhance and beautify our witness.

Be Known for Good Behavior (3:17)

Peter returns to the idea of suffering for doing good (vv. 11,13,16, and 17). He implies that we should not be surprised when suffering happens.

Giving a defense is not a passive calling. It is an active one, a controlled and consistent one. As we do good, it is Christ who is in it, behind it, over it, and for it! Sometimes he leads us into the lions' den (Dan 6) or the fiery furnace (Dan 3) where our good deeds shine all the more brightly for his glory.

Sometimes Christians are the greatest enemy and obstacle to authentic Christianity. When attacked, it is tempting to strike back. But 1 Peter 2:19-24 gives a better model.

> *For it brings favor if, because of a consciousness of God, someone endures grief from suffering unjustly. For what credit is there if when you do wrong and are beaten, you endure it? But when you do what is good and suffer, if you endure it, this brings favor with God.*

> *For you were called to this, because Christ also suffered for you, leaving you an example, that you should follow in his steps. He did not commit sin, and no deceit was found in his mouth; when he was insulted, he did not insult in return; when he suffered, he did not threaten but entrusted himself to the one who judges justly. He himself bore our sins in his body on the tree; so that, having died to sins, we might live for righteousness. By his wounds you have been healed.*

Trust in the Will of God No Matter What (3:17).

God's will is good, as Romans 12:2 makes clear. It is perfect. But it is not easy, and it is not always safe. God's will is not free from suffering. Peter's point is simple and clear. You would not be suffering if it were not God's will. It is one of God's most effective evangelistic secret weapons. The first-century Roman historian Cornelius Tacitus (AD 55–120) records how God put his precious children on glorious display before the eyes of a pagan world through horrible and painful suffering under the crazed emperor named Nero (AD 54–88). He wrote, "Covered with the skins of beasts, [Christians] were torn by dogs and perished, or were nailed to crosses, or were doomed to the flames and burnt, to serve as a nightly illumination, when daylight had expired" (*Tac. Ann.* 15.44). These Christians, and millions of others, have suffered in a way that captured the eyes, the ears, the imagination, and the hearts of an unbelieving world. Their witness could not be denied. No wonder they turned the world upside down (Acts 17:6).

When you do nothing but good, you may still suffer. It is the will of God. According to verse 18, Christ suffered for doing good. Christ suffered and it was God's will. If it is true for him, then it may also be true for me and you. It may provide the perfect opportunity for us to make a case for our faith.

Conclusion

In the song "Living Life Upside Down," Gary Driskell and Karley Worley capture the world in which we find ourselves. We live in an upside-down world. Good is labeled evil. Darkness is loved. People care more about the earth than the unborn. The need for making a case for our faith, with gentleness and respect, has never been greater. The gospel of Jesus Christ, shared with gentleness and respect, will make the case for your faith. It is the truth, and it has power. Go and tell it, and see what God does.

Reflect and Discuss

1. Why must believers think about good and evil (2:13-16,20; 3:13,17) when suffering?
2. Does the command to suffer for righteousness contradict the call to correct injustice?
3. How can the fear of God keep you from fearing people?
4. How does the holiness of Christ embolden you to suffer for righteousness?
5. Why is an ungentle defense contradictory to the gospel?
6. What hope leads Christians to do good when they receive evil?
7. Why might someone ask about your hope if you do good when experiencing evil?
8. Which is more important: how nonbelievers evaluate your conduct or your own self-evaluation?
9. How does Jesus's death explain why God may will someone to suffering?
10. What similarities can you find in Peter's letter and Jesus's Sermon on the Mount?

The Victory of Jesus Christ

1 PETER 3:18-22

Main Idea: Jesus's victory over sin makes it possible for unrighteous people to be saved from their sins.

I. His Work of Reconciliation (3:18)
II. His Work of Proclamation (3:19-20)
III. His Work of Salvation (3:21)
IV. His Work of Ascension (3:22)
V. His Work of Exaltation (3:22)

John Stott wrote the finest book in the past one hundred years on the atoning work of Christ. In *The Cross of Christ,* Stott writes,

> The essence of sin is man substituting himself for God, while the essence of salvation is God substituting himself for man. Man asserts himself against God and puts himself where only God deserves to be; God sacrifices himself for man and puts himself where only man deserves to be. Man claims prerogatives that belong to God alone; God accepts penalties that belong to man alone. (*The Cross of Christ,* 159)

Stott's words find support in 1 Peter. Peter tells us we have been ransomed with the precious blood of Christ (1:18-21). He said that Christ suffered for us as he himself bore our sins in his body on the tree (2:18-25). Now Peter tells us, "Christ also suffered for sins once for all, the righteous for the unrighteous, that he might bring you to God" (3:18). God substituted himself for us on the cross.

The theme of victory rings throughout these five verses. These words would encourage those experiencing suffering and trials. Christ suffered. We will suffer. Christ is victorious, and we will be victorious too.

Through Jesus's death and resurrection, he has saved us. He conquered sin and all evil powers. As Schreiner writes, "Believers have no need to fear that suffering is the last word, for they share the same destiny as their Lord, whose suffering has secured victory over all hostile powers" (*1, 2 Peter*, 180). This is the main idea of the passage. Yet, this is one of the most difficult Bible passages to interpret. The great reformer Martin Luther wrote, "A wonderful text is this, and a more obscure passage than any other in the New Testament so that I do not know for certainty just what Peter means" (*Commentary*, 168). Ray Summers has counted more than thirty variations in interpretations ("1 Peter," 163). Millard Erickson counted 180 different theories (Jobes, *1 Peter*, 239). We will not endeavor to examine the thirty or 180 different interpretations of 1 Peter 3:18-22. We will, however, follow the wise counsel of the Baptist statesman B. H. Carroll: "The spirits in prison: This is a hard passage, let us look at it carefully" ("The Pastoral Epistles," 215). Five aspects of the victory of the Lord Jesus are readily apparent.

His Work of Reconciliation

1 PETER 3:18

Verses 18-22 flow from verses 13-17. Those who "suffer for doing good" (v. 17) should

> draw encouragement from the fact that Christ has suffered and died, and by his death and resurrection has won a stupendous victory over the forces of evil—a victory in which, by virtue of their union with Christ, believers share. (Vaughan and Lea, *1, 2 Peter*, 89–90)

Yes, "Christ also suffered," but his suffering and death are qualitatively different from ours. His was redemptive. He suffered "for sins once for all, the righteous for the unrighteous," the sinless for the sinful. As Hebrews 10:12 says, "But this man, after he had offered one sacrifice for sins forever, sat down on the right hand of God." Peter will note the exaltation of Christ in verse 22. Christ died once. His death was a perfect work. It will never be repeated. Our Savior effected a reconciliation between God and man. His death brings us to God when we repent of our sin and put our faith in Jesus (2 Cor 5:18-21). The sinless Savior did for us what we could not do for ourselves so that we may be brought to God, and we may find him to be not our Judge but our Father (1 Pet 1:2-3).

Jesus died for us "in the flesh." He died bodily, and he was raised from the dead, "made alive by the Spirit" (see 1 Tim 3:16). Schreiner summarizes,

> Even though Jesus suffered death in terms of his body, the Spirit raised (cf. Rom. 8:11) him from the dead. Similarly, those who belong to Christ, even though they will face suffering, will ultimately share in Christ's resurrection. (*1, 2 Peter*, 184)

Those who belong to Christ have the same access to God as Christ. He brings us to the God with whom we have been reconciled (Rom 5:11).

His Work of Proclamation

1 PETER 3:19-20

Now we enter into the interpretive weeds. The text teaches that after the resurrection Jesus went and preached to spirits in prison, whoever they are. These spirits were disobedient in the past, and somehow all of this has a connection to the time of Noah (Gen 6–9). There are dozens of interpretations of these verses, but five are most popular. Good and godly scholars can be found in support of each of these positions. We will use Schreiner's helpful treatment in our survey as well as Vaughan and Lea's (Schreiner, *1, 2 Peter*, 184–85; Vaughan and Lea, *1, 2 Peter*, 95–99).

Option 1	The preincarnate Christ preached through Noah to an evil generation. Augustine (AD 354–430) held this view.
Option 2	Christ descended into hell (*descensus ad inferos*) after his death and proclaimed his victory to those who died during the flood. Some believe he offered this group a second chance to be saved, but there is no biblical support for the second-chance view.
Option 3	Christ proclaimed his victory to Old Testament saints. The phrase "in prison" is used in a "nonhostile sense" for "the place they remained awaiting Christ" (Davids, *First Epistle of Peter*, 138). Calvin held this view.
Option 4	Christ proclaimed his victory over evil angels who had sexual relations with women (see Gen 6:1-4; 2 Pet 2:4-5; Jude 6). These angels were imprisoned since the time of Noah.
Option 5	Christ preached to sinners of the apostolic age through the apostles and others. These are people whose sins are similar to those in Noah's day.

The evidence best supports option 4. The "spirits in prison" refers to fallen, evil angels who committed egregious sins in Noah's time by cohabiting with women, which produced the Nephilim (Gen 6:4). This view has strong support from extrabiblical Jewish writings (Schreiner, *1, 2 Peter*, 187). It also fits well with God's condemnation of evil angels in 2 Peter 2:4 and Jude 6.

After Jesus's death and resurrection, he proclaimed his victory to the evil angels of Genesis 6, who had been imprisoned ever since because of their heinous sin. They had disobeyed God in an extremely evil manner during the days of Noah and were condemned appropriately. How evil were the days of Noah? Only eight persons survived by means of the ark.

The victory of Christ is complete. Demons know it. Sinners need to know it too while they still have time to repent and believe.

His Work of Salvation

1 PETER 3:21

Verse 21 can be easily misunderstood if you glance over it and ignore the context. It is similar to Galatians 5:4, which says, "You have fallen from grace." If you ignore the context, then you may conclude that we can lose our salvation. It does not teach that. Similarly, 1 Peter 3:21 says, "Baptism . . . now saves you." If you ignore the context, then you draw the theologically false teaching of baptismal regeneration. The text does not teach that. Baptism points to our identification with Christ in his bodily resurrection from the dead. Baptism, by analogy ("which corresponds to this"), looks back to the flood and God's saving of eight people (v. 20). In that way baptism "now saves you." How? Not by literally washing away your sins ("not as a removal of dirt from the body") but rather by giving "the pledge [or "appeal" ESV] of a good conscience toward God." All of this is made possible "through the resurrection of Jesus Christ."

The flood of Noah is a type, "a model or pattern for Christian believers" (Schreiner, *1, 2 Peter*, 193). The waters of baptism picture our death (Rom 6:3-5). Schreiner rightly says, "Believers have been saved [by the virtue of our union with Christ] through the waters of baptism" (*1, 2 Peter*, 194). Washing dirt from the body does not save us. The washing of the soul by Christ's victory over death and our union with him does. Calvin writes,

> What then ought we to do? Not to separate what has been joined together by the Lord. We ought to acknowledge in baptism a spiritual washing, we ought to embrace therein the testimony of the remission of sin and the pledge of our renovation, and yet so as to leave to Christ his own honour, and also to the Holy Spirit; so that no part of our salvation should be transferred to the sign. Doubtless when Peter, having mentioned baptism, immediately made this exception, that it is not the putting off of the filth of the flesh, he sufficiently shewed that baptism to some is only the outward act, and that the outward sign of itself avails nothing. ("Commentaries," 118–19)

Peter zeroes in on one purpose of baptism: "The pledge of a good conscience toward God through the resurrection of Jesus Christ." In baptism, based on the death and resurrection of Jesus Christ, a believer appeals to God to give a clear conscience concerning the forgiveness of their sins. As Vaughan and Lea write,

> A "good" conscience is one cleansed by the blood of Christ and assured of acceptance with God. Baptism then is the believer's pledge (or answer) to the work of God in his heart. (*1, 2 Peter*, 101)

The resurrection is God's stamp of approval that the death of Christ takes away the sin of the world (John 1:29). Baptism is our answer and pledge of yes to God. Our conscience is clear. We can now "approach the throne of [God's] grace with boldness" (Heb 4:16).

His Work of Ascension

1 PETER 3:22

The resurrection and ascension are intimately connected. There can be no ascension and exaltation without the bodily, historical resurrection of Jesus Christ from the dead. The one who was resurrected from the dead (v. 21) "has gone into heaven" (v. 22). Resurrection and ascension are a double blow of defeat to the demonic powers (vv. 19-20). The grave could not hold him. He has risen and ascended back to heaven to his Father.

The ascension of our Lord is recorded only in the two-volume work of Luke (Luke 24:50-53; Acts 1:9-11). It is an aspect of our Lord's ministry that is often neglected. However, ten facts mark the ascension as important.

1. **It ended the earthly ministry of Christ.** It marked the end of the period of self-limitation during the days of his life on earth.
2. **It ended the period of his humiliation.** His glory was no longer veiled following the ascension (John 17:5; Acts 9:3,5).
3. **It marks the first entrance of resurrected humanity into heaven and the beginning of a new work in heaven (Heb 4:14-16; 6:20).**
4. **It made the descent of the Holy Spirit possible (John 16:7).** It was necessary for Christ to ascend to heaven in order that he could send the Holy Spirit.
5. **It is the necessary corollary of the resurrection.** That is, it is the abiding proof that the resurrection of Jesus was more than a temporary resuscitation.
6. **It conveyed to the disciples the realization that the appearances, which had occurred at various times over a period of forty days, were at an end.**
7. **It suggested that Jesus was no longer to be perceived by physical sensation but by spiritual insight.**
8. **It provided the occasion for the commissioning of witness and the promise of the Spirit (Acts 1:1-8).**
9. **It provided for our Lord the occasion to bless his church with gifted men (Eph 4:11).**
10. **It provided the occasion for the promise that he would come again (Acts 1:9-11).** (Akin, "The Doctrine of Christ," 419–20)

There is much significance to our Lord's ascension.

His Work of Exaltation

1 PETER 3:22

Jesus has ascended ("has gone into heaven") back to the Father. He is now "at the right hand of God with angels, authorities, and powers subject to him." Ephesians 4:10 says, "The one who descended is also the one who ascended far above all the heavens, to fill all things." Philippians 2:9-11 tells us,

> *For this reason God highly exalted him and gave him the name that is above every name, so that at the name of Jesus every knee will bow—in heaven and on earth and under the earth—and every tongue will confess that Jesus Christ is Lord, to the glory of God the Father.*

Peter alludes to the great messianic song Psalm 110, where the Davidic king, now a King-Priest after the order of Melchizedek, sits at the Lord's right hand. Schreiner instructs us that

> Jesus applied the psalm to himself in his teaching (cf. Matt 22:44; 26:62; Mark 12:36; Luke 20:42-43; 22:69), and the influence of the psalm is pervasive in the rest of the New Testament (Acts 2:34-35; Rom 8:34; 1 Cor 15:25; Eph 1:20; Col 3:1; Heb 1:3,13; 8:1; 10:12). The text circles back to verse 19 emphasizing that angels, authorities, and powers are subjected to Jesus. All three words refer to angels (for "authorities" [*exousia*] see 1 Cor 15:24; Eph 1:21; 3:10; 6:12; Col 1:16; 2:15; and for "powers" [*dynamis*] see Rom 8:38; 1 Cor 15:24; Eph 1:21). (*1, 2 Peter*, 197)

From resurrection to ascension to exaltation, all these marvelous realities flow from the truth, "For Christ also suffered for sins once for all . . . that he might bring you to God" (v. 18). His suffering was great, but his glory is even greater. For those who follow his example and walk in his footsteps, our path may be similar. Great suffering? Possibly. Greater glory? Absolutely.

Conclusion

Martin Luther sums up the victory of our Savior and the victory that is ours because we belong to him:

> This he says to enlighten and strengthen our faith. For it was necessary that Christ should ascend to heaven and become Lord over all creatures and wherever there is a power, that he may bring us thither and make us conquerors. This is now said for our consolation, that we may know all powers, whether they be in heaven or on earth, must serve and aid us, even death and the devil, since all must become subservient to and lie at the feet of the Lord Christ. (*Commentary*, 172)

Reflect and Discuss

1. How does Christ's resurrection prove that it is OK to suffer?
2. How would you be hindered if you did evil in response to suffering?
3. Should the phrase "once for all" stop attempts to earn God's pleasure?
4. How is each person of the Trinity at work in this passage?
5. How can you identify if you are trying to get yourself to God?
6. What value do believers gain from Jesus proclaiming his victory to evil spirits?
7. Which of the ten facts of Jesus's ascension caught your attention? Why did you notice the one you did?
8. How is power a theme for this passage? What kind(s) of power does God display?
9. How is your baptism in Jesus similar to and different from the baptism that happened in Noah's day?
10. Since Jesus's life moved from suffering to power, why should you avoid sin?

Life without Jesus Is a Wasted Life

1 PETER 4:1-6

Main Idea: Because God will judge everyone, followers of Jesus endure suffering instead of returning to a sinful life.

I. A Life without Jesus Is Enslaved to Sin (4:1).
II. A Life without Jesus Is Captive to Human Passions (4:2-3).
III. A Life without Jesus Is Applauded by the World (4:4).
IV. A Life without Jesus Is Not Prepared for Judgment (4:5-6).

Several years ago I had the honor of meeting Rick Barnes, the successful men's head basketball coach of the University of Tennessee. I was with a friend who had been a team manager when coach Barnes was at Clemson. My friend walked up to him and said, "Coach Barnes, you probably will not remember me, but I was a team manager when you were at Clemson." With grace and kindness, Barnes simply said, "That man you knew back then is dead. He died years ago." What Rick Barnes meant was the angry, filthy-mouthed man who idolized basketball no longer existed. He had become a follower of Christ while coaching at the University of Texas. He was a different man from the one he was years ago. He was a new creation in Christ (2 Cor 5:17). He had "finished with sin" (1 Pet 4:1). Sin no longer dominated and ruled his life. Jesus did.

First Peter 4:1-6 builds on 3:18-22, as "Therefore" in 4:1 tips us off. Just as Christ suffered in the flesh (3:18; 4:1), we can expect to suffer in this life (4:1). Following Christ may not always be easy. But when you follow Jesus, you can be assured you will not live a wasted life enslaved to sin (v. 1), human desires (vv. 2-3), and human approval (vv. 4-6). You will live a worthwhile and meaningful life "in the spirit according to God's standards." You will be prepared to meet God at the final judgment (v. 6). You will live the rest of your life "for God's will" (v. 2). Your life will count for eternity. Why is a life without Jesus a wasted life? Peter highlights four reasons.

A Life without Jesus Is Enslaved to Sin

1 PETER 4:1

Peter reminds us that "Christ suffered in the flesh." He suffered in the human, earthly realm. First Peter 3:18 reminds us, "Christ also suffered for sins once for all, the righteous for the unrighteous, that he might bring you to God." Grounded in this truth, he calls us to "arm yourselves also with the same understanding." We need the mind of Christ (Phil 2:5). This is a call to battle. The phrase "arm yourselves" has "military connotations" (Schreiner, *1, 2 Peter*, 199). We must be armed for the battle, especially in our minds, like faithful soldiers (Eph 6:10-20). We must be ready for a life of suffering. "Christ suffered in the flesh," in the body, and those who follow him expect the same. We must have this mind, attitude, and disposition.

This preparedness for suffering is an evidence, a proof, that we are "finished with sin." The ESV translates "ceased from sin"; the NIV, "done with sin." Peter is not speaking of sinless perfection in this life. Rather, sin is no longer our slave master. Sin no longer has a stranglehold on us. Calvin writes, "We are really and effectively supplied with invincible weapons to subdue the flesh, if we partake as we ought of the efficacy of Christ's death" ("Commentaries," 121). In Christ, by virtue of his death and resurrection, we are no longer unrighteous but righteous (1 Pet 3:18). I am no longer lost but saved "by the resurrection of Jesus Christ" (3:21 KJV). The wasted life of being enslaved to sin has been broken. We have been liberated. We have been set free. We are finished with sin. We now live for Christ (Phil 1:21).

A Life without Christ Is Captive to Human Passions

1 PETER 4:2-3

We were once alive to sin. But then we met Christ. Now, we must redeem the time we have left (Eph 5:16). We must "live the remaining time in the flesh [the human body] no longer for human desires, but for God's will" (1 Pet 4:2). There is a new priority in my life, a new master.

We are finished with sin. We are done. The sinful human passions that once enslaved us have been defeated by Christ (3:18-22). Conversion makes a difference. We no longer live for our will, our passions, our desires. We live for God's. Whatever time we have left on earth, it is all God's. Schreiner writes, "Whatever the span of life God grants, believers are to live zealously for God as long as life endures" (*1, 2 Peter*, 202). This life is brief, but our Savior gets it all.

Verse 3 expands the thought of verse 2. We have already spent enough time on a wasted life. "For there has already been enough time spent in doing what the Gentiles [the lost; pagans] choose to do." We have already wasted too much time. Peter describes this time with an abbreviated vice list (cf. 1 Cor 5:10-11; 6:9-10; Gal 5:19-21; Eph 5:3-5). He notes six specific examples of the wasted life. J. D. Charles notes, "The ethical standards could not be more opposite to those that characterize the will of God" ("1 Peter," 343). Note a brief description of each sin.

- "Unrestrained behavior" ("living in sensuality" ESV)—"unbridled lustful excess, conduct that shocks public decency" (Vaughan and Lea, *1, 2 Peter*, 106). Moral constraint is completely absent.
- "Evil desires" ("lust" NIV)—inordinate desires that pervert God's good design, especially as it relates to sexual behavior.
- "Drunkenness"—excessive use of wine or other alcoholic drink.
- "Orgies"—depraved sex parties (Rom 13:13; Gal 5:2), a sin often linked with drunkenness (Schreiner, *1, 2 Peter*, 203).
- "Carousing" ("drinking parties" ESV)—like orgies, carousing is often associated with parties or festivals of a public nature. It points to "excessive acts of eating and drinking . . . vices that characterize the lives of those who are perishing and will not inherit the kingdom of God" (Jobes, *1 Peter*, 263).
- "Lawless idolatry"—("detestable idolatry" NIV) abominable idolatries, idolatries that go beyond the pale and are exceedingly wicked and evil.

Such behavior contradicts God's will. It is vile, warped. It approaches the uncontrolled lust of an animal. How foolish and wasteful is such a life. That life exists party to party. One day the lights will be turned out because the party will be over.

A Life without Jesus Is Applauded by the World

1 PETER 4:4

Peter tells us we are "strangers and exiles" (2:11), spiritual foreigners in this world. Unbelievers immediately notice this when we do not join in "the same flood of wild living" described in 4:4. Their response is twofold: "They are surprised," and "they slander you." Our behavior stuns lost people. They cannot believe we do not join the party of unbridled lust. They believe we should "eat and drink, for tomorrow we die" (1 Cor 15:32). To restrain yourself from sin is deemed crazy. It is called foolish. People with restraint should be mocked, laughed at, ridiculed, and scorned. Schreiner is helpful in putting the first-century situation in context. He writes,

> Pagans are surprised that believers do not participate in what they consider to be normal cultural activities; in response they criticize, defame, and revile believers and thereby also the God they worship. . . .
>
> [U]nbelievers were at first puzzled and then outraged by the failure of believers to participate in activities that were a normal part of Greco-Roman culture. We see such a reaction in Tacitus when he says Christians have a "hatred of the human race" (*Ann.* 15:44). Pagans would feel this way because idolatry was woven into almost every dimension of their lives, from life in the home to public festivals to religious observances and evil social occasions. . . . [P]ublic festivals, in which the gods were venerated, were considered a civic duty in the Greco-Roman world. In particular veneration of the emperor was simply a mark of good citizenship, and the deifying of the emperor was especially pronounced in Asia Minor. Those who failed to participate would be social outcasts just as today American citizens would look with suspicion on those who refused to take the Pledge of Allegiance to the flag. We can imagine that those who did not fit in with the mores of society would be discriminated against in daily life and that they would be the object of abuse. (*1, 2 Peter*, 204)

Schreiner wisely adds, "Sharp words can easily turn to sharp swords" (*1, 2 Peter*, 204). If the world claps for you and praises you, you are probably running with the wrong crowd.

A Life without Jesus Is Not Prepared for Judgment

1 PETER 4:5-6

This life is not all there is. "The Gentiles" (pagans) who don't know God make a crucial error. They mock and slander followers of Jesus (2:21).

But slanderers will give an account to the one (God) who "stands ready to judge the living and the dead" (4:5). Judgment day is coming. No one will escape. The word "account" (v. 5) is courtroom language. The ring of final and eternal judgment sounds out here. Judgment is inescapable. It will happen. You cannot buy your way out of it. There will be no bartering or negotiating at the bar of God. The Judge approaches, and his coming is sooner than most expect (v. 7). Because eternal judgment is certain, we preach the gospel (v. 6). The lost, unbelievers, are not ready. Verse 6 is difficult, but Adrian Rogers sorts it out:

> This is kind of a complicated verse so put on your spectacles: *"For this cause was the gospel preached also to them that are dead"*—now, you say, "Uh-oh, when was the gospel preached to dead people?" When they were alive. He doesn't say, "*is* the gospel preached to those that are dead"; "*was* the gospel preached to those that are dead." They're dead now, but they were alive when they heard the gospel, see. He's not talking about a chance after death. That's not it at all—*"For this cause was the gospel preached [unto] them that are dead, that they might be judged"*—now, watch it—*"according to men in the flesh, but live according to God in the spirit."* (1 Peter 4:6) Now, what happened is this: many of these people were judged by men in the flesh. They looked at these Christians in Peter's time, and they said, "They're not worthy to live." And, they judged them, and they put them to death. And, multiplied thousands of Christians died because they were judged by men in the flesh. The world wrote them off, but they lived unto God in the spirit. It was a time of recognition when those that the world does not recognize God recognizes.
>
> There's another world coming. And so, there's coming a day, a time, of reckoning. There's coming a time of recognition. There is coming a time of reward, for he says they're going to live unto God (1 Peter 4:6). It'll be worth it all when we see the Lord Jesus. And so, some of these people were being put to death, and Peter is telling them, "Don't be afraid. They may judge you. They may even martyr you. They're going to be judged by my righteous judgment, and I'm going to show the difference in their unrighteous judgment of you."

> You know what Jesus said in Matthew 10:28? *"Fear not them which kill the body, but are not able to kill the soul: but rather fear him [who] is able to destroy both soul and body in hell."* ("The Conquering Christian," 553–54; emphases in original)

Believers understand the rest of the story. Death is not the final word. This life is not all there is. Resurrection and judgment are coming. On that day, will your life be seen as worthy or wasted? The answer is of eternal consequence.

Conclusion

As I write these words, I have just learned of the death of a beloved sister and friend in Christ. She was a wonderful colleague and teacher at Southeastern Baptist Theological Seminary and Judson College. She bravely battled cancer for over three years then went home to be with Jesus. Hers was not a wasted life. She understood suffering better than most. She was enslaved to Christ, captive to God's will, applauded by her spiritual family, and prepared to meet Jesus. She was a fountain of wisdom while her life on this earth was drawing to a close. She said this about suffering:

> I believe that God allows bad things in our lives for a reason and that he uses everything, but especially hard things, to draw people to him. I didn't want my suffering to be silent, I wanted it to point to Jesus—the God who hears, the God of all comfort, the God who heals, the God of unfading love. . . . I want my journey to encourage others to taste and see that God is good even when situations are bad; his mercies never fail. ("In Loving Memory")

Her life indeed was not a wasted life. Praises be to God.

Reflect and Discuss

1. How can your former lifestyle remind you to treat others with grace?
2. What will happen to Christians who suffer but have armed themselves with Christ's understanding?
3. Does your "remaining time" feel long or short? What challenges does your remaining time present?

4. How do the vices in verse 3 present themselves as alternatives to suffering?
5. How does a lack of restraint characterize the vices Peter lists?
6. Why does the world applaud a life without Jesus? Why does it not tolerate a life with Jesus?
7. Why would a believer's sinless life be surprising to the world?
8. Since you will give God an account of your life later, how should you examine it now?
9. How should believers relate to the God "who stands ready to judge"?
10. How often do you think about final judgment? How would thinking about final judgment help you follow Jesus?

How to Live in Foreign Territory till Jesus Comes Again

1 PETER 4:7-11

Main Idea: Because Jesus will return, Christians love and serve one another.

I. **Live Wisely and Pray (4:7).**
II. **Love One Another Fervently (4:8).**
III. **Practice Grace-Filled Hospitality (4:9).**
IV. **Serve One Another with Your Spiritual Gifts (4:10-11).**
V. **Glorify God in Everything You Do (4:11).**

Theology is often learned best by the hymns and the songs we sing. Good songs aid memorization and teach us how to "love the Lord your God with all your heart, with all your soul, with all your mind, and with all your strength" (Mark 12:30). Christian truth is wonderfully conveyed through song. This is especially the case when it comes to the doctrine of Christ's second coming. Since I was a small boy, I have loved the song "One Day." The words filled my heart with wonder and worship. The melody causes my spirit to soar. The last stanza points to the coming of our Savior. It fills my soul with joy overflowing.

> One day the trumpet will sound for His coming,
> One day the skies with His glories will shine;
> Wonderful day, my beloved One bringing;
> Glorious Savior, this Jesus is mine!
> (*Baptist Hymnal*, 288)

Peter knows a "fiery ordeal" (1 Pet 4:12) is on the horizon for God's "strangers and exiles" in this world (2:11). Many will suffer. Some will be martyred. Afterall, the lunatic Nero is the emperor. It is essential to keep the imminent return of Christ before their eyes. Only this will sustain them *in* and *through* the "fiery ordeal" on the way. These instructions were critical words for the first-century church, and they are just as crucial for the twenty-first-century church. Peter has five specific words of counsel for our edification in 1 Peter 4:7-11.

Live Wisely and Pray

1 PETER 4:7

We will suffer just as Jesus did (3:18; 4:1,4). Trials are coming. However, don't get depressed or discouraged. "The end of all things is near." Christ will return. The kingdom is coming. The second coming of the Lord Jesus is an important biblical truth. It's imminency is repeated and affirmed again and again in the Bible. Note:

> *Therefore be alert, since you don't know what day your Lord is coming. But know this: If the homeowner had known what time the thief was coming, he would have stayed alert and not let his house be broken into. This is why you are also to be ready, because the Son of Man is coming at an hour you do not expect.* (Matt 24:42-44)

> *Our citizenship is in heaven, and we eagerly wait for a Savior from there, the Lord Jesus Christ.* (Phil 3:20)

> *For you yourselves know very well that the day of the Lord will come just like a thief in the night.* (1 Thess 5:2)

> *Brothers and sisters, do not complain about one another, so that you will not be judged. Look, the judge stands at the door!* (Jas 5:9)

> *But the day of the Lord will come like a thief; on that day the heavens will pass away with a loud noise, the elements will burn and be dissolved, and the earth and the works on it will be disclosed.* (2 Pet 3:10)

> *Look, I am coming soon! Blessed is the one who keeps the words of the prophecy of this book. . . . Look, I am coming soon, and my reward is with me to repay each person according to his work. . . . He who testifies about these things says, "Yes, I am coming soon." Amen! Come, Lord Jesus!* (Rev 22:7,12,20)

There is a complementary truth we must maintain to have a balanced and biblical eschatology. Peter says, "The end of all things is near." He wrote that in the AD 60s. Two thousand years later, Jesus hasn't come. Was Peter mistaken? Not at all. Adrian Rogers put it exactly right: "From the days of Pentecost right up until the present day, we live in an age called the *last* days or the *end* times" ("A Lifestyle of the Last Days," 556; emphasis in original). The following Scriptures support what Pastor Rogers said:

> *And it will be in the last days, says God, that I will pour out my Spirit on all people; then your sons and your daughters will prophesy, your young men will see visions, and your old men will dream dreams.* (Acts 2:17)

> *These things happened to them as examples, and they were written for our instruction, on whom the ends of the ages have come.* (1 Cor 10:11)

> *In these last days, he has spoken to us by his Son. God has appointed him heir of all things and made the universe through him.* (Heb 1:2)

> *Children, it is the last hour. And as you have heard that antichrist is coming, even now many antichrists have come. By this we know that it is the last hour.* (1 John 2:18)

We have been in the last days since Christ's death, resurrection, and ascension. Jesus can come at any time (1 Thess 4:13-18).

So then, what do we do? Peter may have had the words of Jesus, delivered in what we call the Olivet Discourse, ringing in his ears. We find Mark's account in Mark 13. Jesus will return. So, what do we do until that glorious day? Do we set dates? Identify the Antichrist? The false prophet? The mark of the beast? No, here is what we do:

- "Watch out." (Mark 13:5)
- "Be on your guard!" (Mark 13:9)
- "Don't worry beforehand what you will say." (Mark 13:11)
- "Pray." (Mark 13:18)
- "Watch!" (Mark 13:23,33)
- "Be alert!" (Mark 13:33,34,35,37)

We must get our head on straight and think wisely. We must get on our knees before the Lord. "The end of all things is near; therefore, be alert and sober-minded for prayer." Think clearly and be wise. "Be alert" and "be sober-minded" are commands. Peter ties a sense of urgency to prayer. Vaughan and Lea point out the word "alert" can be rendered "be clear-minded"; it is the same word used in Mark 5:15, "where we are told of a demoniac whom Jesus restored to 'his right mind'" (*1, 2 Peter*, 113).

The second word, "sober-minded," speaks of being self-controlled and having a clear mind (Vaughan and Lea, *1, 2 Peter*, 113). Both words are tied to our prayer life. The imminent coming of Christ should impact how we pray. We don't get caught up in an emotional frenzy. We don't become discouraged or depressed because things are tough. As we pray, we pray with a clear mind and self-control. We do not allow persecution, trials, or suffering to rob our minds of the precious truths of Scripture that will strengthen and sustain us. We see things from God's perspective because we know "the end of all things is near." So be alert. Be sober minded in all you do, especially as you go to your knees to talk to your heavenly Father.

Love One Another Fervently

1 PETER 4:8

Peter challenges us to be alert and sober minded (v. 7). He wants us to have our spiritual act together. He also wants our hearts to be right. In verse 8 he urges us, "Above all, maintain constant love for one another." The NASB has, "Keep fervent in your love for one another." We can paraphrase Peter's charge this way: if you have to put anything first, be sure to passionately and continually love one another.

Peter has already addressed the essential nature of love in 1 Peter 1:22 and 2:8. The church must continually and fervently fan the flames of love for one another. We must recall the words of our Lord in John 13:35: "By this everyone will know that you are my disciples, if you love one another." The gospel gives me the power to love people I don't like. Better than that, the gospel gives me the power even to love my enemies (Matt 5:43-44).

Peter observes that "love covers a multitude of sins." He draws upon Proverbs 10:12: "Hatred stirs up conflicts, but love covers all offences." James 5:20 says something similar in the context of evangelism (or restoration of a sinning brother or sister). Peter certainly is not saying our love for others can atone for sin. Nothing in Scripture teaches that. Only the blood of Christ can atone for sin. First Corinthians 13:7 illuminates what Peter is saying. Paul writes, "[Love] bears all things, believes all things, hopes all things, endures all things." Love does not shout the sins of others from the rooftop. As Schreiner writes, "Love covers over the wrongs of others, while those who are full of hatred use the sins of others as a springboard to attack them" (*1, 2 Peter*, 213). It has been well said, bitter people do not live better lives; hateful people do not live happier lives. Peter says to be a reconciler, not a talebearer. Be a forgiver, not a grumbler, which brings us to verse 9.

Practice Grace-Filled Hospitality

1 PETER 4:9

Love others with passion and persistence, then "be hospitable" and stop "complaining" ("grumbling" ESV, NIV). Just as you love "one another," show hospitality to "one another." There is a sense of urgency to these words, as "the end of all things is near" (v. 7) and "the fiery ordeal" (v. 12) is just around the corner. Pastor Warren Wiersbe is extremely helpful concerning hospitality when he writes,

> Our Christian love should not only be fervent and forgiving, but it should also be practical. We should share our homes with others in generous (and uncomplaining) hospitality. . . . In New Testament times hospitality was an important thing because there were few inns and poor Christians could not afford to stay at them anyway. Persecuted saints would need places to stay where they could be assisted and encouraged.
>
> Hospitality is a virtue that is commanded and commended throughout the Scriptures. Moses included it in the law (Ex. 22:21; Deut. 14:28-29). Jesus enjoyed hospitality when he was on earth, and so did the apostles in their ministry (Acts 28:7; Philem. 22). Human hospitality is a reflection of God's hospitality to us (Luke 14:26ff). Christian leaders should be "given to hospitality" (1 Tim 3:2; Titus 1:8).
>
> Abraham was hospitable to three strangers and discovered that he had entertained the Lord and two angels (Gen. 18; Heb. 13:2). We help to promote the truth when we open our homes to God's servants (3 John 5-8). In fact, when we share with others, we share with Christ (Matt. 25:35,43). (*Be Hopeful*, 109–10).

Serve One Another with Your Spiritual Gifts

1 PETER 4:10-11

Spiritual gifts are an important subject in the New Testament. The topic appears in four books of the Bible.

1 Cor 12:8-11	1 Cor 12:28	Rom 12:6-8	Eph 4:11	1 Pet 4:11
Word of Wisdom	Apostles	Prophecy	Apostles	Speaking
Word of Knowledge	Prophets	Service	Prophets	Service
Faith	Teachers	Teaching	Evangelists	
Gifts of Healings	Workers of Miracles	Exhortation	Pastors	
Working of Miracles	Helps	Giving	Teachers	
Prophecy	Administration	Leadership		
Distinguishing of Spirits	Kinds of Tongues	Showing of Mercy		
Kinds of Tongues				
Interpretation of Tongues				

Peter provides the most concise list. He groups all the gifts under two categories: speaking and service.

As we love one another and show hospitality to one another, we use our spiritual gifts to serve one another. When God saved us, he gifted us. ("Just as each one has received a gift, . . .") Why did he give us spiritual gifts? To "use it to serve others, as good stewards of the varied grace of God" (v. 10). Our spiritual gifts are not for us; they are for others. They are not for show. They are for service. We are to be good stewards, not pompous superstars.

Our gifts should be exercised for the glory of God. If you are gifted to speak, make sure what you say is grounded in and faithful to the Word of God (v. 11). If you are gifted to serve, do it "from the strength God provides." Spiritual gifts are not natural abilities. They are grace gifts that need God's enablement and strength. When you exercise your gift, God should receive the glory, not you. Karen Jobes shows us how verses 7-11 beautifully fit together:

> There seems to be somewhat of a sequence to Peter's logic in 4:7-11. First, Christians must have a perspective on life that is informed by the understanding that they live in the final stage of God's redemptive work. That realization must be met with a mental state that rightly apprehends this situation so that prayers can take their proper place in the Christian's life. Thinking rightly and praying in a manner consistent with God's redemptive work enables a love for one another that persists even when one is hurt by wrongs within the community. When one has correctly apprehended reality, is centered on prayer, and is able to break the cycle of wrongs, one can also speak words that are consistent with God's revelation and serve others with a strength that he supplies. (*1 Peter*, 279)

Jobes is on target. When the body functions as God intended, we pray wisely, love one another passionately, care for one another joyfully, speak faithfully, and serve humbly. And God gets all the glory.

Glorify God in Everything You Do

1 PETER 4:11

One of my life verses is 1 Corinthians 10:31: "So, whether you eat or drink, or whatever you do, do everything for the glory of God." The verse appears in a series of commands on how we use our bodies for the glory of God. Peter uses similar words as a glorious doxology to conclude 1 Peter 4:7-11. How we pray, love, and serve one another has one goal in mind: "so that God may be glorified through Jesus Christ in everything."

God has provided the wisdom and strength for ministry. "The provider is always the one who is praised" (Schreiner, *1, 2 Peter*, 215). Whatever good we do in the church and in this world, the power and strength came from Jesus. He deserves the glory, not us. Basking in that truth, Peter can only worship by writing, "To him be the glory and the power forever and ever. Amen." I would simply add, "Praise God from whom all blessings flow" ("Doxology," *Baptist Hymnal*, 668).

Conclusion

The end is near. It could come any day, including today! We began our study with a verse from a song on the second coming of King Jesus. Let us conclude the same way. The final stanza of "It Is Well with My Soul" by Horatio Spafford serves us well.

> And, Lord, haste the day when the faith shall be sight,
> The clouds be rolled back as a scroll,
> The trump shall resound and the Lord shall descend,
> Even so, it is well with my soul.
> (*Baptist Hymnal*, 447)

Reflect and Discuss

1. Do you feel as if "the end of all things is near"?
2. How should Christians live since "the end of all things is near"? What characterizes the person living as if the end is "delayed"?
3. What does an end-time preparation look like according to Peter?
4. How are your prayers affected when you aren't self-controlled or sober minded?
5. Why is prayer an urgent activity?
6. How can we love constantly when sin and suffering exist?
7. Where have you seen love cover sin?
8. What happens when people use spiritual gifts but are devoid of love?
9. Why are believers stewards of God's gift instead of owners?
10. Do you ever substitute yourself as the source, power, or goal of spiritual gifts?

How to Rejoice When You Suffer for Jesus

1 PETER 4:12-19

Main Idea: Expect and be glad that you will suffer like Jesus because you will enjoy blessing like him.

I. **Be Reminded of God's Promises (4:12-13).**
   A. God promises we can expect suffering (4:12).
   B. God promises we can find joy in suffering (4:13).

II. **Be Reminded of God's Pleasure (4:14).**
   A. We are blessed for honoring Christ.
   B. We are helped by God's Spirit.

III. **Be Reminded of God's Parameters (4:15-16).**
   A. We do not honor God when we suffer because of sin (4:15).
   B. We do honor God when we suffer for our Savior (4:16).

IV. **Be Reminded of God's Purging (4:17-18).**
   A. God rightly judges saints first.
   B. God ultimately judges sinners last.

V. **Be Reminded of God's Plan (4:19).**
   A. God is in control: suffering is his will.
   B. God is the creator: he is still working.

Why do righteous people suffer? Christians have pondered this question for centuries. The book of Job is about a righteous sufferer, one who anticipates the ultimate righteous sufferer, Jesus Christ. Following that line of thought, Scottish minister George MacDonald (1824–1905) says, "The Son of God suffered unto the death, not that men might not suffer, but that their sufferings might be like Him" (quoted in Lewis, *The Problem of Pain*, vi). God's choicest fruits that feed and nourish us into Christlikeness are often discovered in his garden of suffering.

Peter writes about immense suffering. The word *suffer* and its variants occur eighteen times in his letter. In 1 Peter 4:12-19 the word occurs four times. Suffering "tests" us (v. 12). It allows us to fellowship "in the sufferings of Christ" (v. 13). It allows us the opportunity to "glorify God" (v. 16). Suffering for "the name of Christ" (v. 14) is "God's will" in order to increase our faith in the God who is a "faithful Creator" (v. 19). God uses suffering to make us more like Jesus. God uses pain for our good and his glory. C. S. Lewis called suffering God's "megaphone" (*The Problem of Pain*, 81). What is God shouting to us in these eight verses?

Be Reminded of God's Promises

1 PETER 4:12-13

Charles Spurgeon said, "Men will never be great in theology until they are great in suffering" ("The Christian's Heaviness and Rejoicing," 461). In other words, to think rightly about our God requires that we attend the school of suffering. Verses 12-13 teach us two important lessons as we begin our education.

God Promises We Can Expect Suffering (4:12)

The phrase "Dear friends" ("Beloved" ESV) signals a new section (see 2:11), though the theme of suffering is not new. Peter commands, "Don't be surprised." What should not surprise us? "When the fiery ordeal ["fiery trial" ESV] comes among you to test you." Peter may be drawing from Malachi 3:2-3. "For he will be like a refiner's fire. . . . He will purify the sons of Levi." This "fiery ordeal" is likely not a reference to the Neronian persecution Christians suffered in Rome in AD 64. First Peter was almost certainly written before then. This is general suffering all Christians experience for following Christ.

This "fiery ordeal" is sent by God "to test you." It is not "as if something unusual were happening to you." This is how God works. Suffering proves our faith and demonstrates its genuineness. Vaughan and Lea write, "Peter wanted his readers to see that God was permitting them to suffer for a purpose, that purpose being the refining of their faith and the overall discipline of their life" (*1, 2 Peter*, 118). James 1:2-4 speaks similarly and says,

> *Consider it a great joy, my brothers and sisters, whenever you experience various trials, because you know that the testing of your faith produces endurance. And let endurance have its full effect, so that you may be mature and complete, lacking nothing.*

Suffering is not unusual. God has multiple plans for using it in our lives.

God Promises We Can Find Joy in Suffering (4:13)

Don't be caught off guard by trials when they unexpectedly knock down the doors of your world, turning upside down the routines of life. "Instead, rejoice as you share in the sufferings of Christ" (v. 13). Once again Peter draws upon the atonement of Christ and his sufferings on our behalf (3:18; 4:1). In 1 Peter 2:21 he wrote, "For you were called to this [suffering], because Christ also suffered for you, leaving you an example, that you should follow in his steps." Because we follow Christ, we fellowship with him in his sufferings. Our sharing in his sufferings is not redemptive. Our sufferings progressively are purifying (v. 17). They are preparatory. Sharing in the sufferings of Christ prepares us "so that you may also rejoice with great joy when his glory is revealed," when Jesus comes again. Calvin comments,

> Hence, then, is the whole consolation of the godly, that they are associates with Christ, that hereafter they may be partakers of the glory; for we are always to bear in mind this transition from the cross to the resurrection. ("Commentaries," 134)

First the suffering. Then the glory. "The first is mingled with grief and sorrow, the second is connected with exultation" (Calvin, "Commentaries," 134). So "rejoice" and "rejoice with great joy." The glory of the second coming is on the way. Our suffering, we will discover, will be worth it.

Be Reminded of God's Pleasure

1 PETER 4:14

Peter specifies the suffering (2:12; 3:9,17; 4:4). We are known for being followers of Christ, so we do not receive the applause of the world. "You are ridiculed for the name of Christ." We may be maligned, slandered, insulted, mocked, and made fun of because of our devotion and dedication to King Jesus. How are we to evaluate what we are experiencing? Peter has two words of encouragement.

We Are Blessed for Honoring Christ

If we are ridiculed for the name of the Lord Jesus Christ, we are "blessed." God has "counted [you] worthy to be treated shamefully on behalf of the Name" (Acts 5:41). Jesus's words in Matthew 5:10-12 could be in the back of Peter's mind when he wrote these words:

> *Blessed are those who are persecuted because of righteousness, for the kingdom of heaven is theirs. You are blessed when they insult you and persecute you and falsely say every kind of evil against you because of me. Be glad and rejoice, because your reward is great in heaven. For that is how they persecuted the prophets who were before you.*

God honors those who honor him.

We Are Helped by God's Spirit

We are blessed "because the Spirit of glory and of God rests" on us. Verse 14 is trinitarian through and through. The Old Testament source is Isaiah 11:1. The world ridicules us, and God gives us more of himself through his Spirit to sustain us. The Spirit that rested on Jesus now rests on us (Schreiner, *1, 2 Peter*, 223). Alan Stibbs is our help and teacher at this point:

> Jesus was sealed from above as God's Christ—He was anointed—by the coming to rest upon Him of the Spirit of the Lord (see Jn. i. 29-34; cf. Is. xi. 2, lxi. 1). So, His people, who bear His reproach and suffer for His Name, are owned as His by a special anointing or manifestation of the Spirit of God. Similarly in Old Testament times the tabernacle or temple was marked as God's dwelling place by the coming of the *shekinah* or "glory" of the Lord, symbolically visible as a pillar of cloud or fire (see Ex. xxxiii.9, 10, xl. 34, 35). It is such special manifestation by God of His Presence with His people of which the persecuted are here assured (cf. Jn. xiv. 23). (*First Epistle General*, 160)

Suffering may make us feel that God has forgotten us. But his Spirit doesn't leave. It rests on us. So we endure all name-calling, public shaming, and disadvantage the world has because they only increase our blessing.

Be Reminded of God's Parameters

1 PETER 4:15-16

Verses 15-16 are a study in contrast. They are not difficult to understand. Verse 15 describes the ways of an unbeliever. Verse 16 describes the Christian and, once more, his or her suffering.

We Do Not Honor God When We Suffer Because of Sin (4:15)

Suffering for sinning is not commendable. If we suffer for doing wrong, we deserve to suffer. Peter makes his point with a short list of four egregious sins. These are illustrative and not exhaustive. Peter admonishes his readers not to suffer for murder, thievery, evildoing, and meddling ("as one who defrauds others" CSB footnote). Warren Wiersbe notes,

> We noted before that not all suffering is a "fiery trial" from the Lord. If a professed Christian breaks the law and gets into trouble, or becomes a meddler into other people's lives, then he ought to suffer. (*Be Hopeful*, 118)

Sin deserves to be punished in this life and the life to come (v. 18). Even if we do not commit these sins in action, it is still sin if we commit them in our hearts (Matt 5:21-26).

We Do Honor God When We Suffer for Our Savior (4:16)

"But if anyone suffers as a Christian, let him not be ashamed but let him glorify God in having that name." We bear the name "Christian." We bear witness to him wherever we can and whenever we can. Our witness is not always well received. In fact, most of the time it is not. How do we respond? Do we grow quiet? Do we deny that we follow Christ, compromise our witness and convictions, or act like we are ashamed of Christ? God forbid! Don't be ashamed of Christ. Be proud of Christ! "Glorify God in having that name." Confess him. Honor him. Praise him. Boast in him (Gal 6:14; Phil 1:26; 3:3). Follow the wisdom of that old song sung by missionaries for decades: "I'll tell the world that I'm a Christian" (*Baptist Hymnal*, 368). Tell the whole world that you are a Christian. Enjoy the honor, joy, and glory that will come with bearing his name.

Be Reminded of God's Purging

1 PETER 4:17-18

Verse 17 begins with the word "for," making connection to the previous verses. Verses 17-18 may startle us at first. Believers can rest, though.

God Rightly Judges the Saints First

The future has invaded the present. Peter declares, "For the time has come for judgment to begin with God's household." The breath of God's judgment is blowing across the world. No one will escape. The language of the verses reflects temple language (Ezek 9; Mal 3). Believers, "God's household," experience judgment first through pruning and purifying. Their judgment, as the saved of verse 18, is a judgment of mercy, grace, and sanctification. It is also a judgment of fiery purifying and severe pruning. Our salvation is not to be taken for granted. We are the righteous because of our union with Christ. We have been "saved with difficulty," by the skin of our teeth as we say. The story of the salvation of Lot from Sodom (Gen 19:15-26) provides a perfect picture. Never presume on your salvation. Our salvation and sanctification required the brutal death and shed blood of God's Son.

God Ultimately Judges Sinners Last

Christians have been saved, and their suffering is sanctifying. Tragically, the unsaved anticipate a different suffering, a suffering of eternal judgment and damnation. Those who "disobey the gospel of God"—"the gospel of God . . . concerning his Son" (Rom 1:1-3)—have rejected their only hope. "What will become of the ungodly and the sinner?" They will receive what they deserve. Peter alludes to Proverbs 11:31, which reads, "If the righteous will be repaid on earth, how much more the wicked and sinful." The judgment of unbelievers is certain, eternal, and horrific. Revelation 20:11-15 calls it the lake of fire and the second death. It is conscious and it is forever. What will become of the ungodly and sinners? We really don't have the words to describe how terrible it will be. That is why we preach the gospel, taking it to all people that they might be saved.

Be Reminded of God's Plan

1 PETER 4:19

Those who suffer for faithfulness to Christ can rejoice. They are experiencing a difficult, but genuine, blessing of God. They experience his presence in a special way. Suffering provides the privilege to glorify God in the name of Jesus. God also uses suffering to purify us. He prepares his church for the glorious return of Christ. All of this is the will of God, as verse 19 makes clear. So, don't worry. God has got this.

God Is in Control: Suffering Is His Will

Peter begins verse 19 with the phrase "so then" ("therefore" ESV). Verse 19 sums up the argument that began in verse 12. It provides a summation of what began all the way back in 1 Peter 3:17. If we suffer for Christ, it is "according to God's will." He planned it, and he has a purpose in it. Romans 12:2 teaches us that God's will is "good, pleasing, and perfect." Schreiner comments, "All suffering passes through his hands (cf. 3:17), . . . nothing strikes a believer apart from God's loving and sovereign control" (*1, 2 Peter*, 229). With God there are no accidents, only divine appointments. There may be pain in your suffering, but there is also purpose in your suffering. There is a plan. That plan is perfect.

God Is the Creator: He Is Still Working

Suffering for Christ is God's will. He purposed it. He planned it. Therefore, "entrust [yourself] to a faithful Creator while doing what is good." Remember the sufferings of Christ. He perfectly fulfilled the Father's will, doing good in Gethsemane and suffering on the cross. He is our example to follow. Trust God, your faithful Creator, every step of the way. Keep doing what is good and right. He is at work with you and in you.

Calling God "a faithful Creator" draws attention to his sovereignty and power over all things, including suffering. Calling him faithful reminds us we can trust him, depend on him, know he will be there and give us exactly what we need in that moment. John Piper concludes this section of 1 Peter by writing,

> In all Christian suffering Satan is seeking to devour faith (1 Peter 5:8-9). God is seeking to test and refine faith (4:12). God's great purpose in all our suffering will be accomplished when we do what Jesus did in the agony of the cross when he cried out (Luke 23:46), "Father, into your hands I entrust my spirit." He entrusted himself to a faithful Creator. According to 2 Corinthians 1:9 God's purpose in suffering is to cause us to rely no longer on ourselves but utterly on him who raises the dead. ("The Holy Spirit Will Help You Die")

God is not finished creating. He will continue making you into Jesus's likeness and will mold and shape your suffering so that it becomes an eternal blessing.

Conclusion

The words of "I'll Tell the World That I'm a Christian" are a wonderful and fitting conclusion to this study. The first stanza reads:

> I'll tell the world that I'm a Christian—
> I'm not ashamed His name to bear;
> I'll tell the world that I'm a Christian—
> I'll take Him with me anywhere.
> I'll tell the world how Jesus saved me,
> And how He gave me a life brand new;
> And I know that if you trust Him,
> That all He gave me He'll give to you.
> I'll tell the world that He's my Savior,
> No other one could love me so;
> My life, my all is His forever,
> And where He leads me I will go.
> (*Baptist Hymnal*, 368)

Reflect and Discuss

1. How has God used suffering as a megaphone to teach you?
2. If fire removes impurities from gold, what impurities does the "fiery ordeal" of suffering remove from your life?
3. How does your view of suffering change when you know God uses it to test you?
4. How does a tested faith honor God?
5. What might stop Christians from expecting suffering?
6. What benefits does suffering produce *in* and *for* the believer?
7. What does the resurrection of Jesus teach you about the goal of suffering?
8. Why should you not take your salvation for granted?
9. How does God's coming judgment reshape how bad you view suffering to be?
10. How does judgment provide justice for suffering believers?

Shepherding the Savior's Sheep

1 PETER 5:1-4

Main Idea: Pastors must shepherd God's people with Christlike motives, love, and gentleness.

I. There Is Encouragement for the Servant of God (5:1).
- A. Let it come from your partners in service.
- B. Let it come from your perception of the Savior.
- C. Let it come from your participation in salvation.

II. There Are Expectations for the Servant of God (5:2-3).
- A. Shepherd God's people (5:2).
  1. Remember the flock is God's possession.
  2. Remember the flock is under our protection.
- B. Serve God's People (5:2-3).
  1. Serve willingly (5:2).
  2. Serve eagerly (5:2).
  3. Serve humbly (5:3).

III. There Will Be an Exaltation of the Servant of God (5:4).
- A. It comes from the chief Shepherd.
- B. It consists of a crown of splendor.

On October 2, 1840, a man named Dan Edwards was ordained as a missionary to the Jews. On that occasion, the Scottish minister Robert Murray M'Cheyne (1813–1843) would charge him,

> Remember you are God's sword, His instrument—I trust a chosen vessel unto Him to bear His name. In great measure, according to the purity and perfection of the instrument, will be success. It is not great talents God blesses so much as great likeness to Jesus. A holy minister is an awful weapon in the hand of God. (Bonar, *Memoir*, 241–42)

The call to the ministry is a great and holy calling. Those who are God called and scripturally qualified for this assignment do not have to wonder what God expects of them. Four texts paint a clear portrait of what the "chief Shepherd" (v. 4), the Lord Jesus, expects them to be and to do:

- Acts 20:17-38: Paul's address to the Ephesian elders at Miletus
- 1 Timothy 3:1-7: Paul's instructions to Timothy
- Titus 1:5-9: Paul's instructions to Titus
- 1 Peter 5:1-4: Peter's instructions to elders among the "chosen . . . exiles" of the Diaspora (1:1)

Thirty years ago, in David Wells's classic *No Place for Truth*, Wells drew attention to the drop in social status that ministers held. He noted,

> In a recent study measuring social prestige, on a scale from one to one hundred, minister ranked fifty-second, cheek by jowl with factory foremen and the operators of power stations. (*No Place for Truth*, 113)

Unfortunately, things have not improved. In an article for Lifeway Research titled "Americans' Trust of Pastors Hovers Near All-Time Low," Aaron Earls reports that the most trusted professions are the following:

- Nurses 89%
- Doctors 77%
- Pharmacists 71%

Pastors trailed far behind, coming in seventh out of fifteen professions, with only 39% of people giving pastors high marks for honesty.

1. Nurses (89%)
2. Medical doctors (77%)
3. Grade-school teachers (75%)
4. Pharmacists (75%) [sic]
5. Police officers (52%)
6. Judges (43%)
7. **Clergy (39%)**
8. Nursing home operators (36%)
9. Bankers (29%)
10. Journalists (28%)
11. Lawyers (21%)
12. Business executives (17%)
13. Advertising practitioners (10%)
14. Car salespeople (8%)
15. Members of Congress (8%)

This dilemma has been caused by many factors. One important factor is an identity confusion among church leaders. Pastors have forgotten *who* they *are* and *what* they *do*. Many pastors see themselves more as managers and organizers than pastors and ministers. Many strive to excel in flashy programs, creative worship, counseling the congregation, raising money, providing administrative direction, and ministering to children and youth while keeping senior citizens happy.

Many have set aside the priority to be ministers of the *Word*, who are "correctly teaching the word of truth" (2 Tim 2:15), and ministers of our *Lord*, who understand they are shepherds, not ranchers. Church elders are pastors, not CEOs.

Churches throughout our country and among the nations vary radically in culture, atmosphere, and worship style. But they *must* have biblical ministers who lead them. Churches need faithful men who shepherd the Savior's sheep.

First Peter 5:1-4 is a crucial text for pastors who lead the churches of the "chief Shepherd" (v. 4). We should read it against the backdrop of Ezekiel 34, which chastises the unfaithful shepherds. "I am against the shepherds," God said (Ezek 34:10). Peter helps us see who a pastor is and what a pastor does. Peter also brings together the three key words for leaders of the local church: elder (Gk *presbuteros),* overseer (Gk *episkopos*), and pastor (Gk *poimēn*). The terms are interchangeable and refer to the same office of spiritual leadership. "Elder" is in the plural; there should be more than one elder in the local church. Peter gives three exhortations to the men who occupy this important office in the Lord's churches.

There Is Encouragement for the Servant of God

1 PETER 5:1

The context of this passage is "glory through suffering." Peter warns his readers of a "fiery ordeal" that will come to test them (4:12). He pleads with them not to be ashamed when they suffer but to glorify God as faithful Christians (4:16). He challenges all believers to "entrust themselves to a faithful Creator while doing what is good" (4:19). Now he addresses how the elders should lead the church.

Several encouragements are discussed in 5:1. They come from three sources: our partners in service, our perception of the Savior, and our participation in salvation. Peter writes to those who are undergoing suffering and trials. The madness of emperor Nero, who burned Rome in AD 64 and blamed it on the Christians, may have found its way to the outer edges of the empire (1:1). The local churches needed to be encouraged and instructed by their leaders. They needed to be fed and led by their pastors, their elders. These men must rejoice as they share in Christ's sufferings (4:12) and as they commit themselves to God in doing good (4:19).

Let Your Encouragement Come from Your Partners in Service

Peter begins by exhorting. He encourages the "elders" of the churches. The word translated "elder" (Gk *presbuteros*), from which we get our word "presbyterian," signifies the office of a church leader. It was a word of respect normally bestowed upon an aged and mature man of "prudence, gravity, and experience" (Calvin, "Commentaries," 143). It became a term of respect, honor, dignity, and esteem that the office itself requires. Peter encourages these men as a "fellow elder," as one involved in the same calling, experiencing the same trials, and given the same responsibilities. He does not pull rank as an apostle or speak with condescension. He stands shoulder to shoulder with them. He is one of them and one with them. He understands the challenges of ministry, and he can empathize with their responsibilities and their difficulties.

To be an effective and successful pastor, you need the encouragement of others. There is no place for a Lone Ranger in the ministry. You need the support of those walking the same path as you. You need others and they need you.

Let Your Encouragement Come from Your Perception of the Savior.

The word translated "witness" (Gk *martus*) identifies one who has seen something, who speaks of it, and who suffers for it if necessary. Peter *saw* Christ suffer. Whether he was at the cross, we do not know. He did see our Lord as he suffered in Gethsemane, and he was there in the courtyard following his arrest (Mark 14:66). Later, with the other disciples, Peter would see with his own eyes the scars on our Lord's body from his passion (John 20:26-29). Peter would *speak* concerning our Lord's passion, and he would *suffer* for the message he proclaimed. According to tradition, Peter was put to death in Rome, crucified upside down. He had become a faithful witness for his Lord.

Fear is a great silencer. It can shut us up and render us mute. How can we overcome this troubling temptation? We must spend time in the *Word* and *prayer* so that we know the passion and person of our Savior. Draw near to Calvary. Meditate on the cross. It has been well said, "If we would make Christ known to others, we must first know him ourselves."

If we know Jesus, we will speak about him. We will boldly proclaim his gospel. We will be willing, if necessary, to suffer for him.

Let Your Encouragement Come from Your Participation in Salvation.

Peter refers to himself as a "one who shares" ("partaker" ESV), a participating saint of the glory of God that will ultimately and fully be revealed at the second coming of Christ. The hope we have of sharing in God's glory strengthens us during suffering. It sustains us in the monumental task before us. It will keep us in the fight until the end.

For the servant of God, through the agencies of prayer, the Bible, the Holy Spirit, and God's people, we have a foretaste of what heaven's glory will be like forever. We can know now, in a small way, what life with Christ will be like forever in his presence. As Fanny Crosby beautifully wrote, "Blessed assurance, Jesus is mine! Oh, what a foretaste of glory divine!" (*Baptist Hymnal*, 446). As we avail ourselves of these privileges, we will be encouraged as servants of God to serve well and finish well (2 Tim 4:7).

Having laid this foundation of encouragement, Peter now moves to the specifics of the minister's assignment, his job description. Our assignment is simple and twofold: shepherd and serve.

There Are Expectations for the Servant of God

1 PETER 5:2-3

"Elder" (Gk *presbuteros*) denotes the office of a minister. The word translated "feed" (KJV) or "shepherd" (Gk *poimēn*), from which we get the concept of a *pastor* (Eph 4:11), and the word translated "overseeing" (Gk *episkopos*), from which we get the concepts of *bishop* and *episcopal*, describe the function of the minister. All three terms appear elsewhere in the New Testament and together in Acts 20:17-28. These three words are used interchangeably to describe the minister, the spiritual leader of the church. He is an elder, a pastor, and a bishop or overseer.

Shepherd God's People (5:2)

In verse 2, the elder is commanded to feed or "shepherd," to tend the flock. The flock is not his. It's God's. We must never forget that the church belongs to Christ, not us. John Piper puts it like this:

> You elders shepherd the people "whom God purchased with his own blood" [Acts 20:28]. . . . Don't take this work lightly. Don't be casual and cavalier and breezy about this responsibility. ("Who Shall Shepherd the Flock?")

This shepherding is amplified by "overseeing," "exercising oversight" (ESV), or "serving as overseers" (NKJV). A minister of God is to care for the needs of his church. He is to protect and provide. He is to feed and lead. It is an assignment that requires hard work, much personal attention, and spiritual commitment.

After the resurrection of Jesus, our Lord commanded Peter to "feed" and "shepherd" his sheep, knowing that sheep have a tendency to wander aimlessly (John 21:15-17). Without direction they get lost and hurt. They may starve in desolation without the care and protection of the shepherd.

The job of a spiritual shepherd is hard work, and it has many facets. Shepherds *feed* the church the Word of God, *protect* the church from heresy and division, and *evangelize* the lost (2 Tim 4:5). Each of these is related to the ministry of the Word (Acts 6:2-4).

Ministers must first preach and teach their people God's infallible, inerrant Word. This demands study, prayer, and expository preaching—preaching that is book by book, chapter by chapter, and verse by verse.

Second, we must protect and warn our people concerning anyone who would question the total accuracy of the Bible and the essential doctrines of the Christian faith. We guard the body from dogs, wolves, and pigs.

Third, we must do the work of an evangelist, making it a priority to be on mission and to be about the business of leading people to faith in Christ. These are the expectations of the Lord who called us.

As we shepherd God's people, nothing is more necessary than a Word-based, expository preaching ministry. J. I. Packer put it perfectly when he said,

> The true idea of preaching is that the preacher should become a mouthpiece for his text, opening it up and applying it as a word of God to his hearers, talking only in order "that the text may speak itself and be heard, and making each point from his text in such a manner that his hearers may discern how God teacheth it." (Packer, *God Has Spoken*, 28; Packer quotes from *Westminster Directory*, 1645)

Suppose your people handled the Word of God the way you handle the Word of God from your pulpit. What would be the end of that? Suppose they expound it like you expound it, teach it like you teach it, treat Scripture like you treat Scripture. Would that be a good thing or a bad thing for your flock? John Stott sounds the alarm so well at this point:

> We should never presume to occupy a pulpit unless we believe in this God, [the God of the Bible]. How dare we speak if God has not spoken? By ourselves we have nothing to say. . . . Once we are persuaded that God has spoken, however, then we too must speak. (*Between Two Worlds,* 66)

A healthy flock will have a healthy diet of the Word of God.

Serve God's People (5:2-3)

Three phrases in these verses give us a negative and a positive perspective on how a pastor is to serve the church. Each is highly instructive. Peter may have penned these words because the elders in these areas were not practicing these

Serve willingly (5:2). We should serve "willingly," not by constraint or "compulsion." We serve not because we were pushed into it. No, we shepherd God's church willingly. We shepherd voluntarily. We shepherd because we love the work. There is an internal compulsion we cannot deny and would not dare attempt to escape. We will not be lazy, and we will not serve out of fear. We will delight in the work.

There is only one reason to be in the ministry: God called you, and you cannot be happy doing anything else. It is simply the fact that you love doing it. You must do it. You want to do it. With all the pressures that come with being a pastor, you must have the right reason for being in the work. There is an internal willingness and love implanted by God, a love for God and a love for God's people. This is how God would have it.

Serve eagerly (5:2). Money is not our motivation. Greed is not our god. We serve not for the sake of getting rich, which becomes dishonorable or dishonest gain. It is not to advance financially as 1 Timothy 6:7-10 warns. Rather, we are to do our work with a ready mind. We serve "eagerly," with enthusiasm and zeal, with sheer delight, joy, and love for our holy assignment.

Sadness must engulf the heart of God when ministers parade about like celebrities and superstars with pleas for money constantly on their tongue. So many so-called pastors fill the airways and the Internet with a pseudogospel message. This malady is striking closer to home with each passing day. The cause of Christ is brutally marred when men prostitute the gospel for personal gain. Why do so many men leave a smaller church for a bigger one? Publicly, it is God's will. Privately, it was the money. God forbid that the overriding concern of a pulpit committee will ever be, "How much will it take to get you here?"

The Bible does not condemn paying a minister. Ministers were being paid, or this phrase would not be here. A good minister is worthy of double honor (1 Tim 5:17). A church devoted to our Lord should see that its ministers are cared for and provided for, not abused and burdened with financial worries. However, Scripture does condemn the manipulation of the ministry for the gaining of wealth.

Servants of God, you work for the sheer love, joy, and delight of the work of the Lord, not for pay. The acquisition of wealth is never to become your goal. God forbid that you should ever compromise your stand for God because of money. That includes your location of service too! You are to have this attitude: "If I could, I'd work for nothing and work in this place forever." That and nothing less is to be the attitude you must have.

Serve humbly (5:3). Peter closes verse 3 with a strong warning against pride in the ministry. Pastors care for God's church, "not lording it over those entrusted to you, but being examples [models] to the flock." We must avoid the "Diotrephes syndrome" (3 John 9-10). We are not to be dictatorial or authoritarian because of the position with which God has graced us. We are to be a pattern worthy to be copied. We are to cultivate such character and conduct that our life is an example of the one we are following: Jesus (1 Cor 11:1).

In the good old days, when you typed a paper on a manual typewriter and wanted the letter *a*, you smartly pressed down on the *a* key and an *a* appeared on the page. The real *a* was on the slug on the little bar within the typewriter. The typed *a* on the paper was a copy of the real *a*. That which is on the paper is a type.

Your life as a minister of Christ is to be on the paper of your life, a type, a copy of Jesus. Your life ought to look so much like Jesus that your people could legitimately look at you and say, "When I look at him, it is like looking at the Jesus I see in the Bible." You are to be a model for the flock to imitate; you are to set the standard in every area: as a husband, a father, a man of God. You are to love Christ more and the people of God more. You are to witness more, serve more, pray more. It is well said, "The church needs leaders who serve and servants who lead." We cannot lead others where we have not been ourselves.

Peter has examined the encouragements and expectations of the minister. Now he turns to the minister's future exaltation and reward.

There Will Be an Exaltation of the Servant of God

1 PETER 5:4

Verse 4 reveals the giver and the gift of pastoral ministry.

It Comes from the Chief Shepherd

When Jesus "appears" the second time, or better "is manifest," he will come as the chief Shepherd, the arch-Shepherd (Gk *archipoimenos*). Jesus is the *chief* Shepherd (1 Pet 5:4), the *good* Shepherd (John 10:11), and the *great* Shepherd (Heb 13:20). He will be the one to exalt the undershepherds of his flock. He will bless them with the gift of an incorruptible, unfading, and eternal crown of glory.

It Consists of a Crown of Splendor

Jesus will grant to his faithful ministers an everlasting crown of glory. The word "unfading" comes from the Greek work *amaranth*, "a flower whose unfading quality was the symbol of immortality" (Hiebert, *First Peter*, 289).

In Peter's day, men ran in the Olympics to win the victor's prize, a flowery wreath to be worn about the head in triumph and splendor. Yet it was worn for only a short time. It soon wilted and faded. It was corruptible, perishable, and fading. Christian workers may labor for many rewards. Some seek to build personal empires. Others long for the applause of men. Others strive for denominational acclaim and promotion. All of these, like the ancient wreath, will fade, pass away, and vanish. The minister's true reward is future, not present. It is from God, not men. It is imperishable, not perishable. For the faithful minister of Christ, the eternal, unfading crown of glory is reserved. Interestingly, in

Revelation 4:10 the twenty-four elders are on their knees before God, casting forth their crowns of glory before the throne of Jesus. All that they rendered in service on this earth was because of him and for him.

Conclusion

Charles Jefferson, in his classic work *The Minister as Shepherd*, says there are seven basic functions of the genuine shepherd:

1. To love the sheep
2. To feed the sheep
3. To rescue the sheep
4. To attend and comfort the sheep
5. To guide the sheep
6. To guard and protect the sheep
7. To watch over the sheep (*The Minister*, 39–66)

In fulfilling these functions, one sees the centrality and priority of the Word of God. Luther was most certainly correct when he wrote,

> Let us then consider it certain and firmly established that the soul can do without anything except the Word of God and that where the Word of God is missing there is no help at all for the soul. If it has the Word of God it is rich and lacks nothing, since it is the word of life, truth, light, peace, righteousness, salvation, joy, liberty, wisdom, power, grace, glory, and of every incalculable blessing. (Luther, "Freedom of a Christian," 279)

Preach the Word. Shepherd the Savior's sheep. An eternal reward awaits you that you will receive from Jesus himself. What more could the faithful minister want?

Reflect and Discuss

1. If glory follows suffering, why do Christians still fear suffering? How do you overcome this fear?
2. How do you become humble by hoping in a crown of life?
3. How is the church blessed by having elders?
4. How can church members submit? How might that help pastors shepherd well?

5. How does sinful pastoring affect the pastor, church members, and unbelievers? What about faithful pastoring?
6. How does an elder's good example support his teaching?
7. Read the qualifications of a pastor in 1 Timothy 3:1-7 and Titus 1:6-9. Why is character more important than capabilities?
8. What motives lead pastors to domineer? Do these motives always start out sinful? What motives lead church members to resist submitting to elders?
9. Is greed for money an *especially* tempting sin for Western American pastors?
10. How can pastors and church members show humility toward one another?

Humility Is the Way Up, Not Down

1 PETER 5:5-14

Main Idea: Humility, perseverance, and glory mark faithful exiles.

I. Humble Yourselves toward One Another (5:5).
- A. Submit to your leaders.
- B. Wrap yourselves in humility.

II. Humble Yourselves toward God (5:6-14).
- A. Wait on God to exalt you (5:6).
- B. Cast all your cares on God because he cares about you (5:7).
- C. Be sober minded (5:8).
- D. Be alert concerning the ways of the devil (5:8-9).
- E. Know you are not alone in your suffering (5:9).
- F. Rest in God's grace and his promises (5:10-11).
- G. Stand firm in God's grace (5:12).
- H. Rejoice with God's family (5:12).
- I. Rest in God's blessings (5:14).

Humility is one of the most important characteristics that identify a Christian. Sadly, it is absent in most of our lives. Humility is at the heart of possessing the mind of Christ (Phil 2:3-5,8). Let's note the following ten verses:

> *And [if] my people, who bear my name, humble themselves, pray and seek my face, and turn from their evil ways, then I will hear from heaven, forgive their sin, and heal their land.* (2 Chr 7:14)

> *He [the* Lord*] leads the humble in what is right and teaches them his way.* (Ps 25:9)

> *For the* Lord *takes pleasure in his people; he adorns the humble with salvation.* (Ps 149:4)

> *He [the* Lord*] mocks those who mock but gives grace to the humble.* (Prov 3:34)

> *When arrogance comes, disgrace follows, but with humility comes wisdom.* (Prov 11:2)

> *Humility, the fear of the* Lord, *results in wealth, honor, and life.* (Prov 22:4)
>
> *For everyone who exalts himself will be humbled, and the one who humbles himself will be exalted.* (Luke 14:11)
>
> *Therefore, as God's chosen ones, holy and dearly loved, put on compassion, kindness, humility, gentleness, and patience.* (Col 3:12)
>
> *God resists the proud but gives grace to the humble.* (Jas 4:6)
>
> *Humble yourselves before the Lord, and he will exalt you.* (Jas 4:10)

"Humility/humble" appears three times in 1 Peter 5:5-6. How humility works itself out, especially in our relationship to God, is the dominant theme of verses 6-14. C. S. Lewis (1898–1963) calls pride and self-conceit the antithesis of humility. It is "the greatest sin." He writes, "It was through Pride that the devil became the devil: Pride leads to every other vice: it is the complete anti-God state of mind" (*Mere Christianity*, 122). Ouch! This strikes too close to home. Lewis continues, "A proud man is always looking down on things and people; and, of course, as long as you are looking down, you cannot see something that is above you" (*Mere Christianity*, 124). You cannot see God if you are proud. When Lewis addresses humility, he writes,

> [God] wants you to know Him, wants to give you Himself. And He and you are two things of such a kind that if you really get into any kind of touch with Him you will, in fact, be humble—delightedly humble, feeling the infinite relief of having for once got rid of all the silly nonsense about your own dignity which has made you restless and unhappy all your life. He is trying to make you humble in order to make this moment possible: trying to take off a lot of silly, ugly, fancy-dress in which we have all got ourselves up and are strutting about like the little idiots we are . . . the comfort, of taking the fancy-dress off—getting rid of the false self, with all its "Look at me" and "Aren't I a good [person]?" and all its posing and posturing. To get even near it, even for a moment, is like a drink of cold water to a man in a desert.
>
> Do not imagine that if you meet a really humble man he will be what most people call "humble" nowadays: . . . always telling you that, of course, he is nobody. Probably all you

> will think about him is that he seemed a cheerful, intelligent chap who took a real interest in what you said to him. If you do dislike him, it will be because you feel a little envious of anyone who seems to enjoy life so easily. He will not be thinking about humility: he will not be thinking about himself at all. (*Mere Christianity*, 127–28)

Peter has two charges for his readers, which we too would be wise to heed. Both address the importance of humility in the child of God.

Humble Yourselves toward One Another

1 PETER 5:5

Peter has charged pastors not to be "domineering" (ESV) or "lording it over" God's flock; rather, they are to be good examples (v. 3). Pastors should be humble servant-leaders just like Jesus. Humility, however, is not only for pastors. Humility is for everyone. We should all seek the mind of Christ that Paul describes in Philippians 2:3-5:

> *Do nothing out of selfish ambition or conceit, but in humility consider others as more important than yourselves. Everyone should look not only to his own interests, but rather to the interests of others. Adopt the same attitude as that of Christ Jesus.*

As we relate to one another, Peter addresses two specifics.

Submit to Your Leaders

Peter ties his instruction in verse 5 to his counsel to the "elders" (v. 1). Younger members of God's "flock" (v. 2) should "be subject to the elders." They should joyfully and voluntarily submit, showing proper respect to their leaders who have been called by God to this assignment (Vaughan and Lea, *1, 2 Peter*, 125).

Their submission has a good, "profitable" goal in mind, as the author of Hebrews makes clear:

> *Obey your leaders and submit to them, since they keep watch over your souls as those who will give an account, so that they can do this with joy and not with grief, for that would be unprofitable for you.* (Heb 13:17)

Submitting to good and godly leaders is good for everyone.

Wrap Yourselves in Humility

Peter has a second command or imperative for all of God's people. His image recalls our Lord Jesus washing the feet of the disciples the night he was betrayed (John 13:1-20). All believers "should clothe [themselves] with humility toward one another." Hiebert notes that the phrase *clothe yourselves* calls for effective action. The verb, used only here in the New Testament, means to put or tie on "any kind of garment. . . . The picture is that of a slave tying on the apron to serve" (Hiebert, *First Peter*, 292). Serving others is the natural fruit of humility. Peter grounds his command in the wisdom text of Proverbs 3:34: "The Lord resists the proud, but to the humble he gives grace" (LXX). Schreiner puts it well when he writes, "Believers should heed the injunction to be humble because God sets his face against the proud, but he lavishes his grace upon the humble" (*1, 2 Peter*, 238). Vaughan and Lea add, "The imagery [is] that of an army lined up against an enemy. The Almighty, as it were, declares war on the proud!" (*1, 2 Peter*, 126). The proud make God their opponent. The humble have God as their helper and friend.

Humble Yourselves toward God

1 PETER 5:6-14

Humility toward one another is important. Humility toward God is essential. It is multifaceted, as verses 6-14 make clear. Verses 6-11 are filled with words of encouragement, instruction, and assurance. Verses 12-14 conclude the letter with a final greeting and benediction. The theme of humility covers them all like a beautiful blanket of blessing. Nine truths are highlighted.

Wait on God to Exalt You (5:6)

Verse 6 continues the theme of humility. It turns our attention to a humble attitude and disposition toward God. "Humble yourselves" is another command. The position of our humility is "under the mighty hand of God." This is a powerful image with roots in the Old Testament. Kistemaker writes,

> This is Old Testament language that describes God's rule in regard to Israel. God showed his powerful hand in leading the

nation out of Egypt (see, e.g., Exod. 3:19; Deut. 3:24; 9:26,29; 26:8). (*Peter*, 198)

The same "mighty hand of God" that delivered and rescued the Hebrews is with his church. He saw Israel through their times of suffering, and he will do the same for his people today. Yet, he will do it in his time, not ours! At the proper time, he *will* exalt you. We bow down acknowledging his great power and perfect plan, and he will lift us up and exalt us at exactly the right time. Our proof is the cross and the empty tomb (Phil 2:6-11). As Adrian Rogers commonly said, "God is never early, and he is never late. He is always right on time!"

Cast All Your Cares on God because He Cares about You (5:7)

One of the blessings of humility toward God is giving him all our anxieties, all our burdens, and all our cares. We can cast all our anxieties on him because he cares about us. Calvin writes, "As soon as we are convinced that God cares for us, our minds are easily led to patience and humility" ("Commentaries," 149).

The God who loves us and cares about us wants "all" our fears, anxieties, and concerns. The big ones and the little ones. None are too big, and none are too small. "Give all your worries and cares to God" (NLT). You will discover that he gives courage, wisdom, strength, faith, hope, and endurance. Jesus is the burden-bearer; we are burden-givers. Give your cares and concerns to the Savior. He has already borne them all on the cross anyway.

Be Sober-Minded (5:8)

This is the fourth command in our text. *The Message* paraphrase says, "Keep a cool head." The NLT has, "Stay alert!" The CSB and the ESV have, "Be sober-minded" (cf. 1:13; 4:7). Vaughan and Lea write, "Recognition of God's sovereignty and His fatherly care does not negate our responsibility" (*1, 2 Peter*, 127). We must be self-controlled. We must be balanced in our thinking about ourselves and God. We must even think well about the devil. That is Peter's next concern.

Be Alert concerning the Ways of the Devil (5:8-9)

"Be alert" is the fifth imperative. It complements "be sober-minded." If we are balanced and biblical in our thinking, we will be "alert" (CSB), "watchful" (ESV), "awake" (NLV), "vigilant" (KJV). Why? "Your adversary the devil is prowling [continually] around like a roaring [continually] lion, looking [continually] for anyone he can devour." Like Jesus, Peter believed in a real, literal devil (John 8:44).

Peter was aware of the tactics of *diabolos,* our "adversary," our "enemy" (NIV). First, he is constantly on the prowl, restlessly on the move for prey. Second, he is fierce and ferocious, continually "roaring" like a lion to intimidate and strike fear in the hearts of God's people. The imagery of the lion also points to his power and strength. However, he is no match for the Lion of the tribe of Judah (Rev 5:5). Further, suffering is one of his most effective weapons to strike fear in our hearts. The devil is continually looking for those he can eat up and swallow.

The reformer Martin Luther (1483–1546) is well known for his battles with and thoughts on the devil. His words are extremely insightful on this verse:

> Satan is by nature such a wicked and poisonous spirit, that he cannot tolerate anything that is good; it pains him that even an apple, a cherry and the like grow; it causes him pain and grief that a single healthy person should live upon the earth, and if God would not restrain him, he would hurl everything together in ruin. But to nothing is he a more bitter enemy than to the dear Word; because, while he can conceal himself under all creatures, the Word is the only agency that can disclose him and reveal to everybody how [dark] he is. Since then you have God's Word, Peter says, and you cleave by faith to it, you should know beforehand that Satan will be your enemy; and you should know that he is not only a wise, cunning, but also a very wicked, poisonous and powerful spirit; so that he rules and dominates the whole world; and therefore Christ also calls him in John 14:30 the Prince, and Paul in 2 Cor. 4:4 and Eph. 6:12, the God and Ruler of this world.
>
> If now Satan, thy adversary, were far from you, and would let you alone in peace, he would do little harm; but he will not do that. He is not a thousand miles from you, but encircles you and stands by your side, so close to you that he cannot come closer; he does not lie upon a cushion, and sleeps and snores; but he walks about without ceasing day and night; not

that he may joke and play with you, nor because he wishes to see what you are doing; but he is angry and furious, and hungrier than a wolf or lion, and seeks not how to appease his hunger with thy possessions or to do you harm in other ways, inflict wounds upon your body, or beat you with a club, or burn your house and court; but his only purpose is to swallow you whole. He walks about, tries and seeks everything, until at last he causes you to fall; now he attacks you and stirs you to adultery and anger, then to avarice, pride, etc. If he succeeds not in this way he tries with terror, unbelief, etc., to persuade you to let go of the Word of God and to doubt his grace. (*Commentary*, 224)

Luther's words perfectly set the table for the counsel of verse 9: "Resist him, firm in the faith." *Resist* is another command. It calls us to vigilant action and resistance. And how do we do this? The Word of God and the gospel. Remain "firm in the faith." We stay in the Word and in our faith in God. Heed the counsel of James 4:7-8:

Therefore, submit to God. Resist the devil, and he will flee from you. Draw near to God, and he will draw near to you. Cleanse your hands, sinners, and purify your hearts, you double-minded.

Here is an unbeatable strategy to resisting the devil. We do it in God's strength, not our own. Satan will whip us every time if we fight in our own power. If we are standing firm in Christ, his strength, and his Word, Satan will run like a baby kitten because he knows the tomb is empty and the battle has been won.

Luther writes in one of his famous hymns,

And though this world, with devils filled,
Should threaten to undo us,
We will not fear, for God hath willed
His truth to triumph through us:
The prince of darkness grim,
We tremble not for him;
His rage we can endure,
For lo, his doom is sure:
One little word shall fell him.
("A Mighty Fortress Is Our God," *Baptist Hymnal*, 656)

Know You Are Not Alone in Your Suffering (5:9)

One way we resist the devil and stand firm in the faith is by knowing we are not alone and are not the exception. "The same kinds of sufferings are being experienced by your fellow believers throughout the world." Suffering for Christ is not restricted or limited. It is worldwide and intense in certain regions of the world. The top areas of the world for the persecuted church at the time of this writing are North Korea, Somalia, Yemen, Eritrea, Libya, Nigeria, Pakistan, Sudan, Iran, and Afghanistan ("World Watch List 2024"). Suffering in America pales in comparison to what other Christians suffer. Knowing how fellow brothers and sisters are suffering should move us to humility. It should move us to prayer. It should move us to action. Suffering is the norm for many. Casting all our cares on our heavenly Father takes on a new meaning when we suffer for our Savior. It has a promise attached for those who endure it well for Christ's sake.

Rest In God's Grace and His Promises (5:10-11)

Suffering is not forever for the Christian. It is for "a little while" (v. 10). Someday it will end. It will end, never to be experienced again. How do you know? Because "the God of all grace" has "called you to his eternal glory in Christ." Schreiner points out,

> "Grace" is a favorite word of Peter's (1:2,13; 2:19,20; 3:7; 4:10; 5:5,12), and here it means that God is the possessor and giver of all grace. The sufferings of believers are intense, but God's grace is stronger still. (*1, 2 Peter*, 244)

His grace moved God to call us to salvation (1:15). His grace moves God to bestow on us "his eternal glory in Christ."

In comparison to eternal glory, our earthly suffering truly is for only "a little while" (cf. 2 Cor 4:17). How will we endure our suffering and remain true to the end? God will do it! He "will himself restore, establish ["confirm" ESV], strengthen, and support you." The God who saved you will sustain you. He got you into the race, and he will see you get to the finish line (Heb 12:1-2). Peter Davids says this of the four words that conclude verse 10:

> What Peter has done is pile up a number of closely related terms that together by their reinforcing one another give

> a multiple underscoring of the good that God is intending for them and even now is producing in their suffering. (*First Epistle of Peter*, 196)

There is one proper response to what Peter has written: a doxology of praise. "To him be dominion forever. Amen" (v. 11). Martin Luther puts it,

> This is the sacrifice of praise that we Christians should offer to God; for since he does all to commence and to complete our salvation, gives us his beloved Son, sends us the Holy Spirit, who strengthens and comforts us through all our lives, sustains us by the pure doctrine, etc., it is right and proper that the honor and praise be his, whose are the work and the power. Therefore, let him be praised in eternity, Amen. (*Commentary*, 231)

Stand Firm in God's Grace (5:12)

Verses 12-14 conclude 1 Peter. "Verse 12 summarizes the letter as a whole," Schreiner writes (*1, 2 Peter*, 247). The phrase "through Silvanus" (or "Silas"; Acts 15:22,27,32,40; 2 Cor 1:19) may mean Silvanus served as an amanuensis or secretary. He was likely the carrier of the letter. He is a "faithful brother" as Peter "considered him." Peter's brief letter—five chapters in our English versions—was "to encourage" his readers and "to testify that this"—what Peter has written in these five chapters—"is the true grace of God." In this encouragement and trustworthy testimony, we are admonished to "stand firm in it!" We are to listen and heed the words of Peter. His teaching is sound and trustworthy, filled with the grace of God. Stand firm and don't be moved.

Rejoice with God's Family (5:13)

Peter's brothers and sisters in "Babylon" send greetings to Peter's readers. Babylon is symbolic for the city of Rome. Literal, historical Babylon was in ruins at that time. So the name *Babylon* represents an enemy that opposes God (Isa 13–14; 46–47; Jer 50–51). In Revelation 17–18, Rome is in view. Harking back to the description of Peter's audience as "exiles dispersed abroad" (1:1), Schreiner notes,

> The mention of Babylon constitutes another reminder that believers are exiles in their present situation, and the allusion

> to exile under the dominion of Babylon constitutes a bookend between the beginning and end of the letter. (*1, 2 Peter*, 251)

Although we are exiles in this fallen world, we are reminded that we are not alone. We have family all over the world. They too have been "chosen" by God. No barriers. We are family.

"Mark, my son" is John Mark. Though he failed to endure in the first missionary journey with Paul and Barnabas (Acts 13:13), he has been restored (Col 4:10; 2 Tim 4:11). He is with Peter in Rome and will write our second Gospel containing Peter's eyewitness testimony. If anyone understood God's grace, it was Mark, whom Peter loved like a son. In the end, Paul loved and appreciated him too.

Rest in God's Blessings (5:14).

Peter's letter ends on a double note of love and peace. "Greet one another with a kiss of love" parallels Paul's expression of a "holy kiss" (Rom 16:16). This was a common way to greet one another and is still practiced in many parts of the world today. It reminds us of the family love we share in our triune God. We have one Father, one Savior, and one Spirit.

"Peace to all of you who are in Christ" is a fitting conclusion to the letter and the theme of humility. "Peace" recalls 1 Peter 1:2. "In Christ" reminds us that true and lasting peace is found in Jesus (Rom 5:1; Phil 4:7). Where peace reigns, humility is present. If we suffer for Christ's sake, we will love one another, serve one another, and experience peace with God and with one another. We know that "eternal glory in Christ" (1 Pet 5:10) is around the corner. Hallelujah! What a Savior!

Conclusion

John Newton (1725–1807), who wrote the famous hymn "Amazing Grace," writes about humility, "I am persuaded that love and humility are the highest attainments in the school of Christ and the brightest evidence that He is indeed our Master" (Newton and Bull, *Letters*, 39). Humility is indeed the way up in the school of Christ. May we all be good students in this school.

Reflect and Discuss

1. Who do you know that exemplifies humility? How do you perceive humility in them? What do you think motivates them to be humble?
2. How does pride lead to every other vice?
3. How can suffering tempt you to act pridefully?
4. How can serving others kill pride?
5. What desires lead younger believers to resist church elders?
6. Why is humility a requirement to receive grace?
7. How does pride prepare you to be devoured by the devil?
8. What does humble resistance against the devil look like?
9. Why are you unable to strengthen and support yourself in suffering?
10. How does knowing that other Christians suffer encourage you to stand firm?

WORKS CITED

Akin, Daniel. "The Doctrine of Christ." Pages 391–437 in *A Theology for the Church*. Edited by Daniel L. Akin. Rev. ed. Nashville, TN: B&H Academic, 2014.

Baptist Hymnal. Nashville, TN: LifeWay Worship, 2008.

Beare, Francis Wright. *The First Epistle of Peter: The Greek Text with Introduction and Notes*. Oxford: Basil Blackwell, 1970.

Bonar, Andrew. *Memoir and Remains of R. M. M'Cheyne*. Edinburgh: Oliphant, Anderson, and Ferrier, 1883.

Brownson, William. *Tried by Fire: The Message of I Peter*. Grand Rapids, MI: Baker Book House, 1972.

Calvin, John. "Commentaries on the Catholic Epistles." *Calvin's Commentaries Volume XXII*. Edited by John Owen. Grand Rapids, MI: Baker Book House, 1999.

Carroll, B. H. "The Pastoral Epistles of Paul, 1 and 2 Peter, Jude, and 1, 2, and 3 John." Pages 1–334 in vol. 6 of *An Interpretation of the English Bible*. Edited by J. B. Cranfill. Grand Rapids, MI: Baker Book House, 1948.

Chapman, Gary. *The 5 Love Languages: How to Express Heartfelt Commitment to Your Mate*. Chicago, IL: Northfield, 1992.

Charles, J. Daryl. "1 Peter." Pages 275–356 in *Hebrews–Revelation*, vol. 13 of *The Expositor's Bible Commentary*. Edited by Tremper Longman III and David E. Garland. Rev. ed. Grand Rapids, MI: Zondervan Academic, 2006.

Cranfield, C. E. B. *The First Epistle of Peter*. London: SCM Press, 1950.

Davids, Peter H. *The First Epistle of Peter*. 2nd ed. Grand Rapids, MI: Eerdmans, 1990.

Davis, Maggie. "Fueled by Social Media, Gen Zers and Millennials Admit to Overspending on Beauty Products." *LendingTree*. August 28, 2023. https://www.lendingtree.com/credit-cards/study/beauty-spending.

Dever, Mark, and Michael Lawrence. *It Is Well: Expositions on Substitutionary Atonement*. Wheaton, IL: Crossway, 2010.

Earls, Aaron. "Americans' Trust of Clergy Hovers Near All-Time Low." Lifeway Research. January 22, 2021. https://research.lifeway.com/2021/01/22/americans-trust-of-pastors-hovers-near-all-time-low.

Foster, Nathan. *The Making of an Ordinary Saint: My Journey from Frustration to Joy with the Spiritual Disciplines*. Grand Rapids, MI: Baker Books, 2014.

Gaines, Grant. "John Owen's 9 Instructions for Killing Sin." *The Gospel Coalition*. April 25, 2002. https://www.thegospelcoalition.org/article/john-owen-killing-sin.

George, Timothy. "The Priesthood of All Believers and the Quest for Theological Integrity." *Criswell Theological Review* 3 (1989): 283–94.

Heimbach, Daniel. *Fundamental Christian Ethics*. Nashville, TN: B&H Academic, 2022.

Helm, David R. *1–2 Peter and Jude: Sharing Christ's Sufferings*. Preaching the Word. Wheaton, IL: Crossway, 2015.

Hiebert, D. Edmond. *First Peter: An Expositional Commentary*. Chicago, IL: Moody, 1984.

"In Loving Memory: Remembering Dr. Adrian Miles." *Southeastern Baptist Theological Seminary*. Accessed September 4, 2024. https://www.sebts.edu/dr-miles-homegoing.

Jefferson, Charles E. *The Minister as Shepherd: Pastoral Leadership according to the Bible*. Apollo, PA: Ichthus, 2019.

Jobes, Karen H. *1 Peter*. Baker Exegetical Commentary on the New Testament. Grand Rapids, MI: Baker Academic, 2005.

Kaiser, Walter C., Jr. *Toward an Exegetical Theology: Biblical Exegesis for Preaching and Teaching*. Grand Rapids, MI: Baker Academic, 1998.

Kay, D. M. "The Apology of Aristides the Philosopher." Pages 257–79 in *Early Church Fathers: Additional Texts. Ante-Nicene Fathers* 10. Transcribed by Roger Pearse, 2003. Accessed September 4, 2024. https://www.tertullian.org/fathers/aristides_02_trans.htm.

Kelly, J. N. D. *A Commentary on the Epistles of Peter and Jude*. Thornapple Commentaries. Grand Rapids, MI: Baker, 1981.

Kistemaker, Simon J. *Peter and Jude*. New Testament Commentary. Grand Rapids, MI: Baker, 1987.

Kreeft, Peter. *Christianity for Modern Pagans: Pascal's Pensées.* San Francisco, CA: Ignatius Press, 1993.

Lenski, Richard C. H., editor. *The Interpretation of I and II Epistles of Peter, the Three Epistles of John, and the Epistle of Jude.* Minneapolis, MN: Fortress, 1945.

Lewis, C. S. *Mere Christianity.* New York: HarperCollins, 2009.

———. *The Problem of Pain.* New York: MacMillan, 1947.

Linder, Jannik. "Money Spent on Clothes Statistics." *Gitnux,* December 24, 2023. https://gitnux.org/money-spent-on-clothes-statistics.

Lusko, Levi. *Through the Eyes of a Lion: Facing Impossible Pain, Finding Incredible Power.* Nashville, TN: Thomas Nelson, 2015.

Luther, Martin. *Commentary on the Epistles of Peter and Jude.* Edited by Paul W. Bennehoff. Grand Rapids, MI: Kregel, 1982.

———. "The Freedom of a Christian." *Three Treatises.* 2nd rev. ed. Translated by W. A. Lambert. Minneapolis, MN: Fortress Press, 1970.

———. *Letters I.* Luther's Works, Volume 48. Edited by Gottfried G. Krodel. St. Louis, MO: Fortress Press, 1981.

Newton, John, and Josiah Bull. *Letters by the Rev. John Newton: Of Olney and St. Mary Woolnoth. Including Several Never Before Published, with Biographical Sketches and Illustrative Notes.* London: Religious Tract Society, 1869.

Owen, John. *The Works of John Owen.* Edited by William H. Goold. 16 vols. East Peoria, IL: Banner of Truth, 1966.

Packer, J. I. *Concise Theology: A Guide to Historic Christian Beliefs.* Carrol Stream, IL: Tyndale House, 2001.

———. *God Has Spoken.* Downers Grove, IL: IVP, 1979.

———. *Knowing God.* Downers Grove, IL: IVP, 2021.

———. *Rediscovering Holiness: Know the Fullness of Life with God.* Grand Rapids, MI: Baker Books, 2009.

———. "What Did the Cross Achieve? The Logic of Penal Substitution." *Tyndale Bulletin* 25 (1974): 3–45.

Pascal, Blaise. *Pascal's Pensées.* Boston: E. P. Dutton & Co, 1958.

Peterson, D. G. "Holiness." Pages 544–50 in *New Dictionary of Biblical Theology.* Edited by Sinclair B. Ferguson and David F. Wright. Downers Grove, IL: IVP Academic, 2000.

Piper, John. "The Beauty and Behavior of a Godly Woman." Desiring God. May 29, 2015. https://www.desiringgod.org/messages/the-beauty-and-behavior-of-a-godly-woman.

———. "Christ Is Hallowed in Us When We Hope in Him." Desiring God. September 18, 1994. https://www.desiringgod.org/messages/christ-is-hallowed-in-us-when-we-hope-in-him.

________. "Christian Identity and Christian Destiny." Desiring God. April 17, 1994. https://www.desiringgod.org/messages/christian-identity-and-christian-destiny.

———. "The Holy Spirit Will Help You Die." Desiring God. June 10, 1984. https://www.desiringgod.org/messages/the-holy-spirit-will-help-you-die.

———. "Holy Women Who Hoped in God." Desiring God. May 11, 1986. https://www.desiringgod.org/messages/holy-women-who-hoped-in-god.

———. "Make a Case for Your Hope." Desiring God. October 19, 1980. https://www.desiringgod.org/messages/make-a-case-for-your-hope.

———. "Men, Love and Lead Your Wives." Desiring God. May 29, 2015. https://www.desiringgod.org/messages/men-love-and-lead-your-wives.

———. "Slaves of God: Free from All to Honor All." Desiring God. May 29, 1994. https://www.desiringgod.org/messages/slaves-of-god-free-from-all-to-honor-all.

———. "A Sojourn on Earth in Confident Fear." Desiring God. December 12, 1993. https://www.desiringgod.org/messages/a-sojourn-on-earth-in-confident-fear.

———. "What Is Submission in Marriage?" Desiring God. May 29, 2015. https://www.desiringgod.org/messages/what-is-submission-in-marriage.

———. "What the Prophets Sought and Angels Desired." Desiring God. November 21, 1993. https://www.desiringgod.org/messages/what-the-prophets-sought-and-angels-desired.

———. "Who Shall Shepherd the Flock?" Desiring God. April 24, 1994. https://www.desiringgod.org/messages/who-shall-shepherd-the-flock.

———. "Your Calling Is to Bless Believers." Desiring God. September 11, 1994. https://www.desiringgod.org/messages/your-calling-is-to-bless-believers.

Rogers, Adrian. "The Conquering Christian." *Adrian Rogers Legacy Collection: 1 Peter.* Memphis, TN: Love Worth Finding, 2022. https://www.lwf.org/pdfs/21_1Peter.pdf.

———. "A Lifestyle of the Last Days." *Adrian Rogers Legacy Collection: 1 Peter.* Memphis, TN: Love Worth Finding, 2022. https://www.lwf.org/pdfs/21_1Peter.pdf.

Schreiner, Thomas R. *1, 2 Peter, Jude: An Exegetical and Theological Exposition of Holy Scripture.* New American Commentary. Nashville, TN: Holman Reference, 2003.

Shenvi, Neil, and Pat Sawyer. *Critical Dilemma: The Rise of Critical Theories and Social Justice Ideology—Implications for the Church and Society.* Eugene, OR: Harvest House Publishers, 2023.

Shiner, Rory. "In My Place Condemned He Stood: Penal Substitutionary Atonement." The Gospel Coalition | Australia. October 31, 2022. https://au.thegospelcoalition.org/article/in-my-place-condemned-he-stood-penal-substitutionary-atonement.

Smietana, Bob. "Presbyterians' Decision to Drop Hymn Stirs Debate." *USA TODAY.* August 5, 2013. https://www.usatoday.com/story/news/nation/2013/08/05/presbyterians-decision-to-drop-hymn-stirs-debate/2618833.

Spurgeon, Charles Haddon. "The Best Thing in the Best Place." Pages 409–20 in vol. 52 of *The Metropolitan Tabernacle Pulpit.* Pasadena, TX: Pilgrim Publications, 1978.

———. "The Christian's Heaviness and Rejoicing." Pages 457–64 in vol. IV of *The New Park Street Pulpit.* Pasadena, TX: Pilgrim Press, 1859.

———. "Fear Not." Pages 389–97 in vol. 3 of *The New Park Street Pulpit.* Pasadena, TX: Pilgrim Publications, 1981.

Stibbs, Alan M. *The First Epistle General of Peter.* Tyndale New Testament Commentaries. Grand Rapids, MI: Eerdmans, 1960.

Storms, Sam. "10 Things You Should Know about the Christian's Responsibility to Human Government." Sam Storms: Enjoying God. February 10, 2020. https://www.samstorms.org/all-articles/post/article-10-things-you-should-know-about-the-christian-s-responsibility-to-human-government.

Stott, John. *Between Two Worlds: The Challenge of Preaching Today.* Grand Rapids, MI: Eerdmans, 2017.

———. *The Cross of Christ.* Downers Grove, IL: IVP, 2021.

Summers, Ray. "1 Peter." Pages 141–71 in vol. 12 of *The Broadman Bible Commentary: General Articles Hebrews-Revelation.* Nashville, TN: Broadman, 1972.

Thielen, Martin. *What's the Least I Can Believe and Still Be a Christian? A Guide to What Matters Most.* Louisville, KY: John Knox, 2011.

Trueman, Carl R. "When Identity Politics Consumes Theology." *WORLD.* December 9, 2022. https://wng.org/opinions/when-identity-politics-consumes-theology-1670591013.

Vaughan, Curtis, and Thomas D. Lea. *1, 2 Peter, Jude.* Bible Study Commentary. Grand Rapids, MI: Zondervan, 1988.

Wells, David F. *No Place for Truth: Or Whatever Happened to Evangelical Theology?* Grand Rapids, MI: Eerdmans, 1994.

Wiersbe, Warren W. *Be Hopeful: How to Make the Best of Times out of Your Worst of Times.* Wheaton, IL: Victor Books, 1982.

"World Watch List 2024." Open *Doors.* 2024. https://www.opendoors.org/en-US/persecution/countries.

SCRIPTURE INDEX

Jude

Revelation